CHICAGO DAILY
SUN TIMES
THE PICTURE NEWSPAPER

LOOK
BOTH WAYS
BEFORE
CROSSING
STREETS

The Making of Chicago's New Morning Newspaper

REAL CHICAGO

PHOTOGRAPHS FROM THE FILES OF THE CHICAGO SUN-TIMES

INTRODUCTION BY ROGER EBERT

RICHARD CAHAN
MICHAEL WILLIAMS
NEAL SAMORS

A CITYFILES PRESS BOOK

Introduction is separately copyrighted by Roger Ebert.
Two photographs are separately copyrighted by John H. White.

First printing: September 2004
Second printing: January 2005

Edited by Richard Cahan, Michael Williams and Neal Samors.

Produced by Michael Williams and James B. Kirkpatrick of Kirk's Computer Service.

Book designed by Michael Williams and Richard Cahan.

Printed in Canada by Friesens Corporation.

ISBN: 0-9725456-2-X (Softcover)

ISBN: 0-9725456-3-8 (Case)

Front Cover: "The Loop During a Dull Day." Photo by Bill Sturm, 1948

Back Cover: Chicagoans react to the news that Robert F. Kennedy was assassinated.
Photo by Clarence Peters, June 6, 1968

Frontispiece: Opening night of the *Chicago Sun.* 1941

Reprints of the photographs contained in this book are for sale at www.suntimes.com

CONTENTS

ACKNOWLEDGMENTS

The authors would like to thank the *Chicago Sun-Times* for the use of its photographs and its unbridled cooperation. This is a joint publishing project. The *Sun-Times* has offered encouragement and support in the editing process, but has in no way mandated what should be used in the book—and we have valued this editorial freedom. This year marks the 75th anniversary of the start of the *Chicago Times*, a newspaper that merged with the *Chicago Sun* to form the *Sun-Times*. This year also marks the start of a new era in *Sun-Times* history as it moves into new offices. This exceptional archive of photographs and negatives moves with the paper.

In particular, we would like to thank Dan Miller and Jaclene Tetzlaff, who originated the idea. John Cruickshank, Michael Cooke, John Barron, Don Hayner, Nancy Stuenkel, Deborah Douglas, Toby Roberts, Ernie Torres and Dom Najolia made our research possible. Ron Theel and Herb Ballard, keepers of the archive, made us feel comfortable and offered essential clues to worthwhile work. The photo and engraving staff helped gather and prepare photographs in the midst of deadline pressure. Former *Sun-Times* photographers Bob Kotalik, Jack Lenahan, Gene Pesek, Ralph Arvidson, Kevin Horan and Pablo Martinez Monsivais graciously gave their insight into the past. Special thanks go to Tom McNamee, Jim Fleming, Jim Kirkpatrick, Richard Falstein, Linda Loye and Eric White, who provided essential editorial help. Thanks also to the Newberry Library, the repository of Chicago journalism history.

ABOUT THE PHOTOGRAPHS

Most of the photographs in this book were printed from original negatives or scanned from vintage prints. The prints often show the work of retouchers, artists whose job it was to prepare photos for the vicissitudes of 70-line newspaper screens. Retouching, which defined details and softened backgrounds so photographs would pop on the press, looks almost comical today. We have retained these retouching marks because they are difficult to erase and because they harken back to another age of newspapering.

Photos by *Sun-Times* photographers since 2000 were often taken with digital cameras. Digital prints have an entirely new look, just as photographs taken with 35-millimeter cameras look different from images taken with large-format cameras.

A few of these photographs are impossible to accurately date. In that case, we have used the stamped date on the storage envelope of the photograph. Sometimes the stamp indicates when the photograph was used in the paper or when it was received in the newspaper library. In these cases, we have included the word "dated" in our captions.

We have attempted to keep original caption headlines whenever appropriate and have placed those headlines in quote marks.

Photo credits on a few photos are missing because they are unavailable.

We have searched through hundreds of thousands of photographs to tell the story of Chicago. Some of these photographs have graced the pages of newspapers before, but a surprisingly high number of these images have never before been printed or even seen.

INTRODUCTION ROGER EBERT

Most of the photographs in this book were taken on the spur of the moment, in an uncertain situation, with quick and instinctive framing, by photographers who were standing right there whether they were supposed to be or not. Most of them were taken before the era of smart cameras; there was not always time to use a light meter, so f-stops were chosen out of experience and instinct, and the light source was a flashgun and those old flashbulbs that were good for one shot.

My first newspaper job was in 1958, so I grew up around the photographers of those years, who had mastered the strategies of camera handling and bulb replacement and had a symbiotic relationship with their cameras. Those bulbs were hot after they were fired; photographers handled them with handkerchiefs, stuffing them into their coat pockets. The nightmare was when a roll of film had to be replaced just when a perfect shot was happening. There was joy when 35-millimeter cameras came on the market, with 36 exposures a roll; for many photographers, they replaced the Rolleiflex, which loaded with a roll of only 12 pictures. Don't even think about the old Speed Graphics you see in the 1930s gangster movies.

Today's high-speed professional digital cameras would have been unimaginable miracles to the previous generation of newspaper cameramen. But notice, in these pages, how often they and their cameras were in the right place at the right time. The famous shot of Sewell Avery, the Montgomery Ward boss who resisted President Roosevelt and was bodily carried from his office, was not posed—except, we feel, by Avery himself, crossing his arms to look defiant between the two soldiers. Consider, too, the photographer with the imagination to record Al Capone's exit from this world by somehow getting inside the hearse to shoot his coffin as it was removed. Look at the photograph of the Reverend Martin Luther King Jr. being comforted after being stoned in Marquette Park; Larry Nocerino, the photographer, was close enough to catch a stone himself. And ask the photographer how he walked right into Richard Speck's hospital room, and made a photo of the reviled killer, looking pathetic and inconsequential on his bed, his feet hanging off the end.

Where were the photographers? How did they place themselves so well? The low-angle shot of Kennedy and Nixon after their first debate in Chicago captures aspects of their personalities from an unguarded angle. The photographers were there for the split second when Maria Callas screamed at a federal agent, and when Martha Mitchell uncorked the wicked smile that said she knew some things and was gonna spill the beans. And how did Richard Derk find the right floor and window to shoot Spider Dan as he climbed past on his way to the summit of the Sears Tower?

Other photographs here involve not spontaneity, but forethought. The longer you look at the city blocks that were bulldozed to make way for the Eisenhower Expressway, the more you appreciate the sheer brute power of that project. The shot of the woman faced with the pneumatic tubes at Marshall Field's is like a study in commerce running wild; I remember pneumatic tubes in department stores, which shuttled cash and change back and forth between customers and a central cashier, but I imagine this photo will be a mystery, almost an abstraction, to some.

The sad Aladdin surveying the ruins of Riverview says whatever can be said when a beloved place is lost. The twisted girders of the burned-out McCormick Place made a natural composition, and you wonder how many of today's Chicagoans know there was an earlier McCormick Place before the one we have today, and it burned down. Do they remember the tragedy of the Our Lady of the Angels fire? Down in Urbana, where I was growing up in the 1950s, we took daily delivery of the *Chicago Daily News*, and I followed the horror of the Grimes sisters disappearance. The photograph of Mrs. Grimes kneeling at prayer between their two little beds, with the Elvis photos on the wall above, is worthy of Diane Arbus. Nathan Leopold's attorney, Elmer Gertz, looks pleased by his victory, but Leopold looks away, sad, distracted. It's eerie how the shadow of the photographer blocked out reflected light and allowed the camera to see through Elizabeth Taylor's car window at the dedication of Michael Todd's grave. Something like that is not an accident. News photographers know about reflections and shadows and stand where they stand out of long practice.

Images from Chicago history: Ernie Banks hits 500. Michael Jordan rules the NBA. Lenny Bruce is arrested. Marilyn Monroe comes to town—and Frank Sinatra, Grace Kelly and the Beatles. The world comes to a halt on the day they buried JFK, and people gather solemnly in front of TV. The 1968 Democratic convention, and Mayor Richard J. Daley shouting at Abe Ribicoff from the floor and giving employment to legions of lip readers. Emmett Till's funeral. His mother left the casket open so all could see the pitiful state of the body after racists had done their savagery.

And photos from one of the *Sun-Times'* greatest moments: the Mirage series. The paper opened and operated a bar on the Near North Side, using concealed cameras and reporters as bartenders to chronicle the countless ways, big and small, that payoffs and corruption were a fact of life for small businessmen. That series ran every day for a month, to almost unreasonable delight on the part of the paper's staff, and our readers.

These photographs appeared in the *Chicago Sun-Times* (and its predecessors the *Chicago Sun* and the *Chicago Times*), and in the *Chicago Daily News*, our sister newspaper for many years. Some of them appeared in papers I read on the day they were published. I knew many of the photographers, including our Pulitzer winners Jack Dykinga and John H. White. I occasionally found myself peering over shoulders at the City Desk as a sensational new photo was shown around—the day, for example, the *Sun-Times* proved that the "bullet holes" cited by the *Tribune* after the death of Black Panther Fred Hampton were in fact nail heads.

These photographs are moments in time. Today we get most of our news images from television, but it's not the same. TV is always in the process of moving on, and the images flow out of the set and into a void and are lost to time. A photograph says: This happened, and the light that fell upon it was captured by photographers who put themselves in the way of trouble or good fortune to show that it happened. You can count on it.

Roger Ebert is the Pulitzer Prize-winning film critic of the Chicago Sun-Times

Wendell Willkie is struck by an egg in the La Salle Street Station on October 23, 1940. After winning the National Headliner Award, photographer Borrie Kanter wrote: "You set your shutter at 1/50th and your lens opening right—and be dere!"

THE SETTING RICHARD CAHAN

It took about four seconds to take all of the images in this book. But it took dozens of people working seven days a week for more than 60 years to make them.

They are precious.

They look anything but precious. They look tough and gritty and real.

The photographers who took these images were able to do more than simply record what was happening in front of their cameras. They recorded truths—about human life and about the place and times in which these pictures were taken.

This collection encompasses pictures from the *Chicago Times*, the *Chicago Sun*, the *Chicago Sun-Times* and the *Times'* sister paper, the *Chicago Daily News*. The *Sun-Times* and *Daily News* photo staffs were competitors, but the papers shared the same darkroom and filed photos in the same photo library for almost two decades. The *Daily News* closed in 1978, but most of its photographs remain in the *Sun-Times* files.

This book is about modern Chicago, glimpses of the city since the early 1940s when the *Sun* and the *Times* were going head-to-head. Based on the photo archive of the *Chicago Sun-Times*, the book offers a look at Chicago as it battered its way through World War II, endured population booms and busts and transformed itself into the city by the lake we know today. It is based on a collection of prints, negatives and digital files. Some of these photos were easily accessible—filed in alphabetical order by subject or by name in the *Sun-Times* library. Many had long been forgotten—moved out of the way to an attic in the paper's office headquarters at 401 N. Wabash Avenue. All were recently moved six blocks west to the *Sun-Times'* new office at 350 N. Orleans Street.

This is a collection of newspaper moments. We see the city in crisis and celebration. And we see personal highs and lows. Newspaper presses see no gray tones; there are few medium moments in these photographs. We have chosen a range of photos that define Chicago. We look at these pictures—very much out of their original context—with Twenty-first Century eyes. From the wide angle of the years, these pictures combine to show us what's in between. Real Chicago.

• • •

It is one of the great newspaper photos of all time.

Republican presidential candidate Wendell Willkie is struck by an egg as he campaigns in 1940 at Chicago's La Salle Street Station. The photograph, taken by Borrie Kanter, ran on the front page of the *Times* with the headline: "It Shouldn't Happen Here."

The subject of the photograph is Willkie—or so it seems. The headline, which is affixed to the photo, makes it clear that the photograph is about more than the egg-faced Willkie. It is about democracy; it's about Chicago; it's about America.

Ever since Chicago emerged from prairie muck to become the Metropolis of the Midwest, the city has stood for America. Not surprising, really; it's situated between New York and San Francisco, between Indiana and Iowa. Yet, Chicago has always meant more than its boundaries or size might suggest. The fictional Sister Carrie, who symbolized rural America, came here because Chicago was so close and so exhilarating. The real Robert S. Abbott, who founded the *Chicago Defender*, spread the word of Chicago through the Pullman train porters and started a great migration that continues today. Chicago is America's heartland. It is the one city that reflects the whole of the nation.

• • •

Sun-Times photographers are a particular breed. Mickey Rito, Bill Vendetta, Louis Giampa and Johnny Arabinko. These are tough names. Armed with Speed Graphics or Nikons, their job has always been the same: Tell the story. Stand down the third-base line at Comiskey Park or stand tough in the line of fire on West Madison Street. They take their job seriously; they are the public eye. Tomorrow their work will be judged by a half-million people.

GEORGE KOTALIK TRAINED PIGEONS IN 1939 TO CARRY FILM FROM NEWS AND SPORTS EVENTS BACK TO THE OFFICE. SOMETIMES THEY RETURNED. (PHOTO BY BILL PAUER.)

The paper they work for and the photos they take have a style. Ever since its first editions, the *Sun-Times* has been Chicago's meat-and-potatoes paper—put out by tireless, hardworking, big-hearted Grabowskis. The term Sun-Timesman, which of course now includes Sun-Timeswoman, has always connoted a journalist who thought of readers first. The goal every day was to touch a chord—to make readers think, to make readers mad.

"This may sound funny," former *Sun-Times* editor Frank McHugh once said. "But we have always fancied ourselves as missionaries. We want to play a role in the city."

Photographs have always played a crucial part of that mission. Photos—full of life and emotion—are the heart of the paper. Anything can happen in *Sun-Times* photos because each staff photographer knows, like a free safety in football, that he or she alone must make that tackle.

"We are working guys, not artists," said Jack Lenahan, a photographer whose career at the paper spanned the 1940s through the 1990s. "We never came back until we got the shot."

So what characterizes the *Sun-Times* photography department?

Ask the staff, and each one will tell you that that their work is constantly hurried. The *Sun-Times* photo department has always been understaffed. That makes photographers scrappy and resourceful—as well as frustrated. Even on a big story, *Sun-Times* staffers often work alone. But that makes for direct, straightforward pictures, pared-down to their essence.

More important than the hurry is the humanity of the staff. *Sun-Times* photographers, just like reporters, connect with their subjects. "It's a culture that is embedded in all of us," said Tom McNamee, a *Sun-Times* reporter since the early 1980s. For photographers, that culture translates into an unwritten mandate to look for human grace. That is the common thread that binds this work. *Sun-Times* photographs—whether of movie stars or accident victims—most always suggest dignity.

"I never once got up in the morning and thought, 'Oh hell, I have to go to work,'" said Bob Kotalik, who started as a *Times* copy boy and retired almost 50 years later as the *Sun-Times* chief photographer. "I never knew what I was going to do. I could be with the president or Marilyn Monroe."

THE *TIMES* CHRONICLED CRIME NEWS IN THE 1930S: CROWDS JAM THE COOK COUNTY MORGUE IN 1934 TO VIEW JOHN DILLINGER'S BODY AFTER DILLINGER WAS KILLED BY FBI AGENTS OUTSIDE THE BIOGRAPH THEATER. (PHOTO BY ROCCO PADULO JR.)

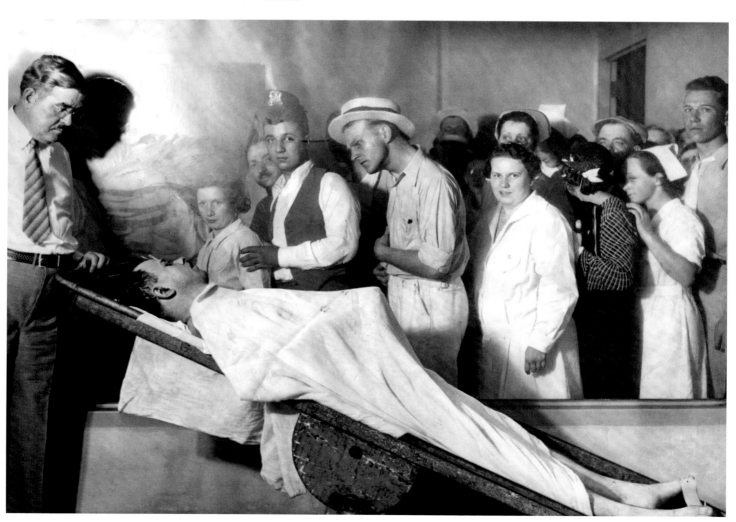

These pages bear witness to changing ideas about news photography. Take a look at camera contests from the 1950s and you can see at an instant that our taste and standards have changed. The constant, of course, is that readers want to see people. We depend on newspaper photographers to get tight enough so that we can see our neighbors' faces. Too shy to look closely at each other in real life, we depend on the camera to let us linger. We want to see ourselves. So that's how a person looks in jubilation. So that's how a person looks in despair.

These pages also show the transformation of press photography from the one-shot Speed Graphic era through grainy 35-millimeter decades to the streaming digital days of today. The *Sun-Times* abandoned large-format cameras in the early 1960s and single-lens reflexes in the late 1990s. Darkrooms, shut down years ago, don't even smell of chemical developer anymore.

But the photographs are a continuum. *Sun-Times* photos—especially those that stand alone without accompanying articles—are like short stories. They are stopped in time. We, as readers, add the beginning of these stories and add the end in our minds. We look at them to soothe us, to challenge us and to teach us.

• • •

The *Sun-Times* was conceived in the Tribune Tower.

In 1927, *Chicago Tribune* business manager Samuel E. Thomason asked the paper's owner, Colonel Robert R. McCormick, why Thomason's new contract did not specify his responsibilities.

"For 250,000 dollars a year, you'll do as you're told," McCormick reportedly told his underling. So Thomason tore up the contract and walked out. Within two years, he started the *Chicago Times*, a paper he modeled after the *New York Daily News*, which he'd helped establish a decade earlier. The *Times* even included a camera in its logo and declared itself Chicago's Picture Newspaper. On September 3, 1929, Thomas sat in his offices at 15 South Market Street and exhaled as his trucks headed out carrying the first edition.

"Well," he sighed, "There goes the last of what was once $2 million."

In that first edition, Thomason and *Times* editor Richard J. Finnegan wrote that photographs would be the key to the new illustrated daily because "picture papers say so much in such a little space that they are popular and successful." The *Times* would be a "paper for folks," they wrote, and promised readers that they could read the 2-cent tabloid from cover to cover in 20 to 30 minutes a day. "In a year that will add from five days to a week to your time for other important things."

Finnegan believed in the power of photographs.

"Nothing in any newspaper of that period convinced an important group of our solid citizens on the facts of life as then being lived so thoroughly as the picture of misery under Wacker Drive," he said of a photo showing men asleep near Michigan Avenue. "Here was misery just outside his lower door, but William Wrigley didn't know about it till he saw that picture."

Finnegan hired *Tribune* photographer Mike Fish as his chief photographer and gathered an experienced staff of newspaper photographers—many from the defunct *Chicago Journal*. Some were hired because they could move around the city with confidence. Bob Rankin was a auto salesman; Bill Pauer was a motorcycle messenger and Dante Mascione was a musician. Fish was succeeded in the late 1930s by Tom Howard, who was known for using a secret ankle-mounted camera to photograph Ruth Snyder, the first woman ever to die in the electric chair.

September 3, 1929, turned out to be an milestone day in U. S. history because that was the day the stock market reached its all-time high before the Depression. One month and 33 editions later the market would crash, the Roaring Twenties would be over and America would never be the same.

Readership rose during the 1930s, but advertising dropped. The *Times* managed to hold its own because of its lavish use of photos and because of the ingenuity of managing editor Lou Ruppel, who demanded "Lots of sock!" When Edward VIII abdicated the throne to marry Wallis Warfield Simpson in 1936, the paper ran a full page photo of the happy couple on Page 1 with the headline "Long Love The King!" The paper made news—with words and pictures. In 1935, the *Times* sent a reporter posing as a patient into the Kankakee State Hospital and bannered "Seven Days in the Madhouse!" In 1937, the paper sent reporters and photographers around the country to document Nazis in America. And during the mid-1940s, two *Times* reporters found information that led to the release of convicted cop killer Joseph Majczek. Their work inspired the 1948 James Stewart movie "Call Northside 777."

JOESEPH MAJCZEK WALKS THROUGH STATEVILLE PRISON ON NOVEMBER 26, 1944. "SOME DAY HE HOPES TO WALK OUT THE FRONT DOOR FREE," WROTE PHOTOGRAPHER MEL LARSON. THE EFFORT BY TWO *TIMES* REPORTERS HELPED PROVE THAT MAJCZEK WAS INNOCENT OF KILLING A CHICAGO POLICE OFFICER.

Many stories survive about these bawdy years of Chicago journalism, and some of them are even true. One of the best is about *Times* photographers George Emme and Bob Rankin, who sneaked into a suburban Evanston hospital to photograph the conductor involved in a 1936 El crash. The injured trainman was under tight police guard. The Timesmen, disguised in priests robes, convinced the police that their service was needed by the patient. Once inside, Emme removed his camera from his cassock and took one shot. The *Times* got its picture.

• • •

Marshall Field III, whose grandfather had founded the Marshall Field's department store, returned to the city to take up his family's legacy in the 1940s. Field had woken from a self-described upper-crust stupor during the mid-1930s with a calling to create publications that would improve the world. In 1940, he established the newspaper *PM*, a radical New York City daily that accepted no advertisements. He came to Chicago in 1941 to create a more traditional newspaper.

The *Sun* was conceived to skim off the *Tribune's* morning readership, champion President Franklin D. Roosevelt's New Deal policies and challenge Colonel McCormick's isolationist sentiment. Buoyed by a pledge from 100,000 Chicagoans that they would buy the new paper, Field recruited editors from around the country. The *Sun* was created on the run. The paper's first employees were hired in September 1941; its printing contract was signed in October. The paper produced its first dummy issues in late November. Eighteen photographers were hired, but they were forced to change film in closets at first because darkrooms were not yet finished.

The *Chicago Sun* appeared December 4, 1941—three days before Pearl Harbor. Production of the first issue was witnessed by the mayor, the governor, boxer Gene Tunney and newsreel crews. When Volume 1, Number 1 came off the press, Marshall Field held it up as if he had just given birth and declared: "Well, Chicago, here it is. I hope you like it."

The demand for the paper was astounding. Close to 900,000 copies of the 2-cent broadsheet paper sold on its first day. Most dealers were emptied out by 10 a.m. But the start of war put a quick end to one of the main reasons for the *Sun's* existence—its call for intervention. By the time the smoke cleared above the USS Arizona, the *Tribune* had joined the ranks, proclaiming on its masthead "Our Country, Right or Wrong."

The *Sun* flourished and floundered during World War II. Readership was high because Chicagoans relished reading the latest war news, but wartime restrictions and the economy limited advertising. The *Sun* fought on many fronts, resisting a government order to cut newsprint consumption and challenging an effort by the *Tribune* to block its membership in the Associated Press. Without the wire service, the paper had to depend even more on its own reporters and photographers.

The expectations that surrounded the *Sun* when it opened were never realized. Three months after its debut, Milton Mayer wrote in *The Nation* that the *Sun* was neither good nor bad. He criticized the paper for lacking direction and distinction. It was, he wrote, a crusader without a cause.

"The *Sun* doesn't know the town and hasn't touched it," Mayer wrote. "Chicago is a slugging town and a sentimental town. The *Sun* hasn't waded into anything yet."

By the end of the war, the *Sun* was shriveling. Circulation was down to 300,000 and the paper was saddled with high payments to the afternoon *Chicago Daily News* for use of its presses. Meanwhile, the *Times* had slowly climbed to a circulation of more than 400,000. It was a crafty paper, directed by editors who knew the city. In 1947, Field bought the *Times* for $5.3 million and announced he would print the new *Sun* as a tabloid on the *Times'* presses at 211 W. Wacker Drive. At first, Field ran two papers, but he combined the Sunday papers in 1947 and combined the daily papers in 1948, forming the *Sun & Times* and eventually the *Sun-Times*. Field's new paper was printed around-the-clock. By the early 1950s, when the *Sun-Times* became a strictly morning publication, the paper had a staff of 22 photographers and photo-technicians. That figure has remained fairly constant over the last half century.

In 1957, all of the negatives from the *Sun* and *Times* were moved over to the *Sun-Times'* new office at 401 N. Wabash Avenue. The building was the height of modernity, with dustproof darkrooms and new high-speed presses. Two years later, Marshall Field IV purchased the *Chicago Daily News* and moved that paper to Wabash Avenue. Field donated all of the *News'* glass plate negatives, primarily taken during the first three decades of the Twentieth Century, and

JOHNNY BRATTON KNOCKS OUT ROBERT EARL IN A BOXING MATCH AT THE CHICAGO STADIUM ON JANUARY 19, 1945. THIS WAS CARMEN REPORTO'S MOST FAMOUS PHOTOGRAPH, KNOWN AS "RIGOR MORTIS."

hundreds of thousands of negatives through the 1950s to the Chicago Historical Society. The *Daily News* did keep its archival prints, and integrated them into the *Sun-Times* photo library.

• • •

Newspaper photography changed drastically during the 1960s. The relationship between press photographers and police was altered when the Summerdale Police District scandal broke in 1960 and crooked cops became the focus of newspaper photographers.

New technology also transformed newspaper photography. The traditional press cameras, which produced single 4-inch-by-5-inch negatives, were phased out in the early 1960s at the *Sun-Times* and other papers around the country. The cameras were replaced by 35-millimeter cameras, which produced smaller negatives in a roll. Many *Sun-Times* staffers welcomed the change to the lighter, more versatile cameras. A few had trouble making the switch and at least one chose retirement over learning new tricks.

The 1960s also launched a whole new generation of photographers. The first photographers at the *Sun-Times*, like those at other city papers, had not been trained or schooled in photography. Few went to college; they generally came out of the ranks of copy boys. By the mid-1960s, new hires were often generally college educated—some even going to photography school. It was time for this new generation to reshape photography.

• • •

Much from the old school remains. The names of 1940s-era *Sun-Times* photographers still grace the doors of darkrooms. Present-day photographers continue to cruise the city and retain a second sense of where to hang out by listening to the back talk of police scanners. Cell phones have replaced radio phones with whipsaw antennas. Digital cameras and laptop computers have replaced 35-millimeter cameras. But the process remains the same.

Those who shot for the *Sun-Times* retain battle scars from their work.

Bob Kotalik is haunted by seeing the bodies of 92 school children and three nuns come out of the Our Lady of the Angels fire. "I felt terrible when I saw the parents out there yelling and crying and screaming because they knew their kids were dead. I didn't like making those pictures," he said.

And Jack Lenahan sometimes walks with a limp—the aftermath of being beaten by more than a dozen police officers during a 1968 antiwar demonstration in the Loop.

Before his death in 1996, photographer Carmen Reporto told his family he wanted no service. "I covered too many funerals and wakes in my life to want one myself."

So, are these photographers artists? If you had suggested that to old-timers such as Louis Okmin, you might get a punch in your face. Now, a few *Sun-Times* photographers quietly talk about their lives as visual artists. They work for a newspaper, but they certainly lead determined lives of art—using their cameras to communicate. And they certainly produce their share of art.

SUN-TIMES PHOTOGRAPHERS HIT THE STREET IN 1956: LOUIS GIAMPA (FROM LEFT) LARRY NOCERINO, BILL PAUER, BOB KOTALIK, CARMEN REPORTO, HOWARD LYON, RALPH WALTERS, BILL STURM, BILL KNEFEL, DAVE MANN AND JOE KORDICK. (PHOTO BY JACK LENAHAN.)

THE FORTIES

"WORLD WAR II INTERRUPTED LIFE AT THE *CHICAGO SUN* AND *CHICAGO TIMES*, JUST AS IT DID ALL OVER," SAID BOB KOTALIK, WHO STARTED AS A COPY BOY WITH THE *TIMES* IN 1944. AT LEAST 11 *TIMES* PHOTOGRAPHERS AND SIX *SUN* PHOTOGRAPHERS JOINED THE ARMED FORCES DURING THE WAR. KOTALIK SERVED WITH THE ARMY SIGNAL CORPS FOR TWO YEARS.

ONCE BACK, KOTALIK'S FIRST BIG ASSIGNMENT CAME IN 1946, WHEN HE WAS SENT TO COVER RIOTING AT THE AIRPORT HOMES HOUSING PROJECT ON THE SOUTH SIDE.

"PHOTOGRAPHY. IT JUST CAME TO ME," HE SAID. "I NEVER TOOK ANY LESSONS; I JUST STARTED TO SHOOT."

PRESS PHOTOGRAPHERS DURING THOSE YEARS HAD GREATER ACCESS TO THE NEWS THAN TODAY'S PHOTOGRAPHERS. POLICE SLOWLY WALKED SUSPECTS PAST WAITING PHOTOGRAPHERS. SOME CRIMES WERE EVEN RE-ENACTED FOR FILM. AND PHOTOGRAPHERS WERE FREE TO TAKE PICTURES IN CRIMINAL COURT—OFTEN BEHIND A PRESIDING JUDGE.

THOSE WERE FAR DIFFERENT DAYS, KOTALIK SAID. "WE USED TO GO ON WALKS WITH PRESIDENT TRUMAN EVERY MORNING WHEN HE CAME TO TOWN."

NEWSBOYS HAWK THE FIRST EDITION OF THE TABLOID *CHICAGO SUN* ON OCTOBER 6, 1947.
PHOTO BY DAVE MANN.

PEARL HARBOR NIGHT. PHOTO BY GEORGE KOTALIK, DECEMBER 7, 1941
JAPANESE CONSULATE EMPLOYEE DESTROYS DOCUMENTS HOURS AFTER JAPAN'S ATTACK ON PEARL
HARBOR. A *TIMES* PHOTOGRAPHER OUTWITTED GUARDS AT THE NORTH MICHIGAN AVENUE CONSULATE TO
MAKE THE PICTURE.

LEFT: DESECRATED BY A SWASTIKA. PHOTO BY JOHN ARABINKO, JULY 25, 1941
JAKE POLLACK SHOWS A BRICK THROWN THROUGH THE WINDOW OF HIS NORTHWEST SIDE STORE.

IN THE ARMY NOW. PHOTO BY VERN WILLIAMS, JUNE 4, 1942
DRAFTEES RIDE THE MADISON STREET STREETCAR AFTER ROLL CALL AT A LOCAL DRAFT BOARD.

'SUNSHINE AND CLOUDS.' MARCH 24, 1941
GRACE SULLIER (LEFT) AND ELEANORE ROCKWOOD SEE OFF DEPARTING ILLINOIS TROOPS AT DEARBORN STATION.

Taking cover. Photo by George Kotalik, April 15, 1942
Children in the 1300 block of South Keeler Avenue find shelter as soon as air raid siren sounds.

Left: Ready for blackout. August 12, 1942
The city goes dark as it holds a 30-minute blackout test. "It looked as if somebody had turned over a giant inkwell," said crib keeper Edward F. Warner. This photo looks north on La Salle Street.

V FOR VICTORY. PHOTO BY BORRIE KANTER, JULY 19, 1942
MARVA LOUIS, WIFE OF WORLD BOXING CHAMPION JOE LOUIS, LEADS DRILLS AT COMISKEY PARK.

LEFT: WOMEN MAN THE FACTORIES. PHOTO BY MEL LARSON, JUNE 16, 1943
MARIE PASTIAK HANDS HAMMER TO ANITA SCHWARTZ AT CARNEGIE ILLINOIS STEEL IN SOUTH CHICAGO.

A BIG SENDOFF. PHOTOS BY AL RISSER, AUGUST 31, 1943
DOUGHNUT RELAY AT THE WASHINGTON BOULEVARD USO CENTER.
RIGHT: WALTER MILLER AND DOLORES DEBILZAN CURTSY AND BOW.

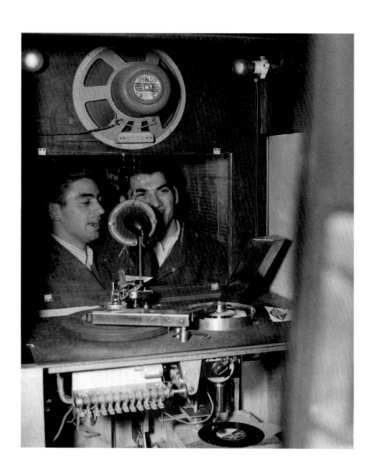

A DAY AT PENNYLAND ARCADE. PHOTO BY JOSEPH L. ZACK, NOVEMBER 21, 1942

SUNDAYS ON MAXWELL STREET. PHOTOS BY RUSSELL HAMM, OCTOBER 24, 1942

Not a New Dealer. Photo by William Pauer, April 27, 1944
GIs carry Montgomery Ward boss Sewell Avery from his office in labor dispute.

Right: Larger than life. 1945
Portrait of President Franklin Delano Roosevelt is prepared outside City Hall.

'KISSES FOR A PRIVATE.' PHOTO BY GEORGE KOTALIK, MAY 8, 1945
PURPLE HEART WINNER WALTER PLATT IS REWARDED BY ALINE AULD
(LEFT) AND PAULINE REED.

RIGHT: FALSE V-E DAY. APRIL 29, 1945
CHICAGOANS AT RANDOLPH AND DEARBORN STREETS CELEBRATE THE
FIRST FLASH OF NEWS—LATER PROVED FALSE—THAT NAZI GERMANY
HAD SURRENDERED.

ALMOST HOME. PHOTO BY BORRIE KANTER,
MAY 8, 1945
CORPORAL JOHN RIDGE, PASSING THROUGH
CHICAGO, WATCHES V-E CELEBRATION FROM
AN ASH CAN ON FRANKLIN STREET NEAR
MADISON STREET.

SPOILS OF WAR. PHOTO BY BILL KNEFEL, OCTOBER 22, 1947
SERVICE FOR WORLD WAR II MARINE HARRY LEWANDOWSKI AT ST. ADALBERT CEMETERY IN NILES. HIS REMAINS,
ALONG WITH MANY OTHERS, WERE RETURNED FROM PACIFIC BATTLEGROUNDS FOR REBURIAL.

LEFT: PRAYER FOR RETURN. PHOTO BY AL WESTELIN, AUGUST 14, 1945
MRS. JOSEPH HERTELENDI PAUSES ON V-J DAY TO THANK GOD FOR PROTECTING HER TWO FIGHTING SONS.

WISHFUL THINKING. OCTOBER 8, 1945
MANAGER CHARLIE GRIMM CELEBRATES GAME 6 WORLD SERIES VICTORY. THE CUBS LOST THE SERIES.

RIGHT: DERBY DAYS. PHOTOS BY MICKEY RITO, NOVEMBER 11, 1947
ROLLER DERBY MATCH BETWEEN TEAMS FROM CHICAGO AND NEW YORK AT THE COLISEUM.

'WITH THE GREATEST OF EASE.' PHOTO BY CHARLES GEKLER, DATED APRIL 19, 1942
THOROUGHBRED CHOCOLATE MAID PRANCES DURING MORNING WORKOUT AT SPORTSMAN'S PARK.

RIGHT: RAIL BIRDS. PHOTOS BY CHARLES GEKLER, SEPTEMBER 14, 1946
SPECTATORS WATCH THE END OF THE GOLD CUP RACE AT HAWTHORNE RACETRACK.

Date night in Riverview. Dated August 25, 1945
Left: Marjorie Holmen's skirt takes to the air in Aladdin's Castle. Above: She tumbles in the rolling barrel with her friend, Carter von Rautenkranz.

Fountain drinks. November 1946
A slower pace comes to a world finally at peace.

Left: 'Queen of mighty basement console.' Dated November 26, 1947
Helen Sarros works new pneumatic tube system to take cash at the Marshall Field's store.

LOOKING DOWN ON CHICAGO

TOP: EAST CHICAGO STEELWORKS, OCTOBER 9, 1947. (PHOTO BY DAVE MANN.) ABOVE: THE UNION STOCKYARDS, OCTOBER 9, 1947. (PHOTO BY CHARLES GEKLER.) LEFT: STATE AND RANDOLPH STREETS ABOVE THE MARSHALL FIELD'S CLOCK IN 1946. (PHOTO BY RALPH FROST.)

'The Loop during a dull day.' Photo by Bill Sturm, November 4, 1947
From under the El tracks, looking south from State and Lake streets.

'To work at dawn.' Photo by Bill Sturm, 1948
A work wagon at 13th Street and Newberry Avenue.

AL CAPONE IS BURIED. PHOTO BY JOHN MENDICINO, FEBRUARY 4, 1947
THE GANGSTER'S BRONZE COFFIN, WITH $30,000 WORTH OF FLOWERS, IS REMOVED FROM A HEARSE AT MOUNT OLIVET
CEMETERY AFTER BEING BROUGHT BACK TO CHICAGO FROM FLORIDA. HIS BODY WAS LATER MOVED TO MOUNT CARMEL
CEMETERY IN SUBURBAN HILLSIDE.

RIGHT: 'TEN SECONDS BEFORE FATAL LEAP.' PHOTO BY JOHN ARABINKO, DECEMBER 22, 1947
LAST WORDS OF A DISTRAUGHT PATRICIA BRODY FADE FROM HER LIPS AS SHE ENDS HER ARGUMENT WITH POLICE. MOMENTS
LATER, THE WOMAN BROKE AWAY AND PLUNGED TO HER DEATH OUT AN APARTMENT WINDOW. POLICE NEVER KNEW WHY.
[CROP MARK AND RETOUCHING PAINT HAVE BEEN LEFT ON THE PRINT.]

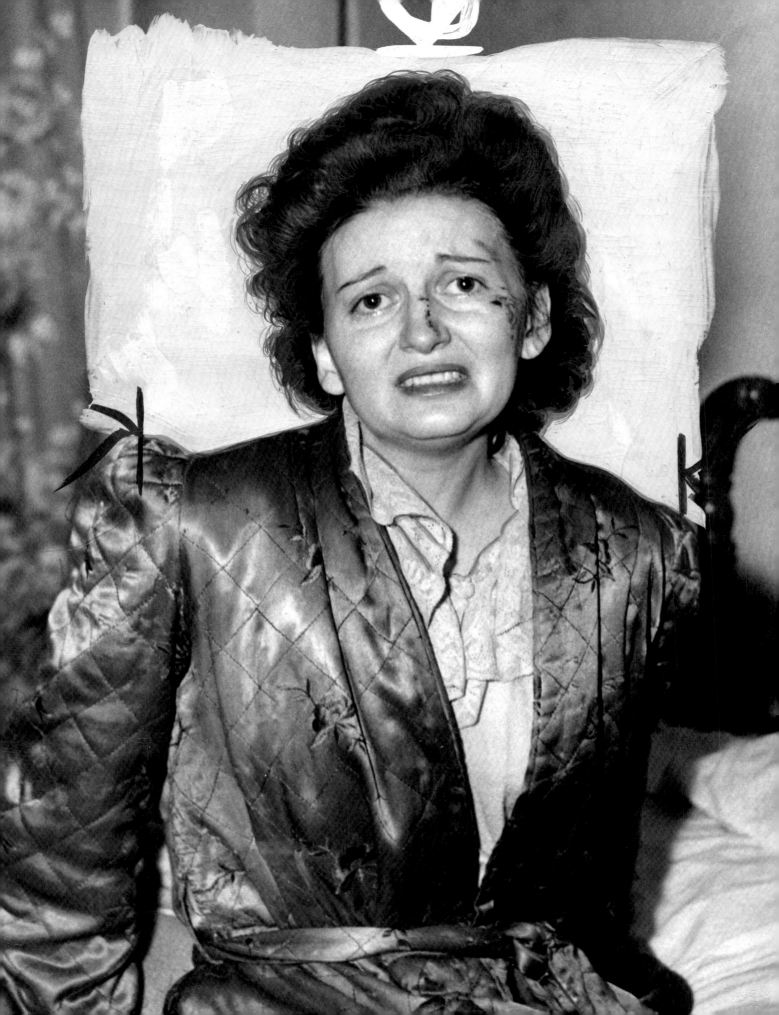

WILLIAM HEIRENS' NIGHTMARE. PHOTO BY MATTHEW ANDERSON, JANUARY 7, 1946
INVESTIGATORS FIND DISMEMBERED BODY PARTS OF 6-YEAR-OLD SUZANNE DEGNAN IN A SEWER SOUTH OF
HER EDGEWATER HOME. SHE WAS FOUND MISSING THAT MORNING.

RIGHT: THE ACCUSED. PHOTO BY BILL KNEFEL, JULY 3, 1946
WILLIAM HEIRENS, WHO CONFESSED TO DEGNAN'S MURDER, IS PHOTOGRAPHED BY POLICE. AFTER
BRUTAL INTERROGATIONS, THE UNIVERSITY OF CHICAGO UNDERGRADUATE ALSO ADMITTED MURDERING
TWO OTHER WOMEN. HE NOW PROCLAIMS HIS INNOCENCE. "I CONFESSED TO LIVE."

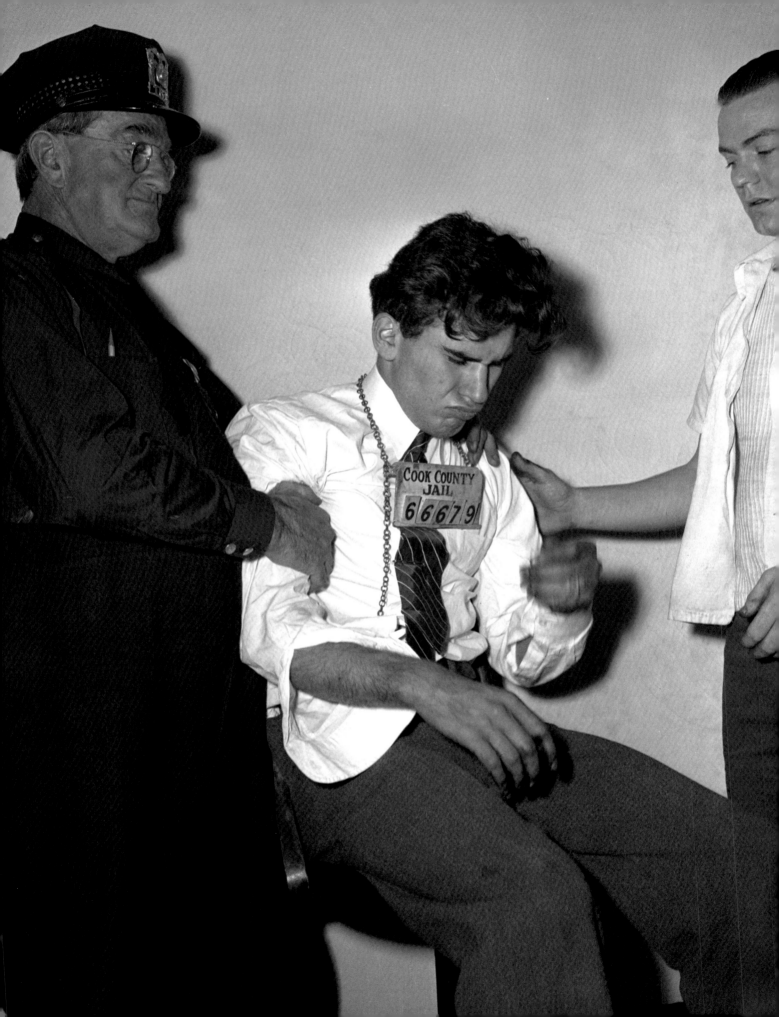

Gypsy funeral. Photo by John Mendicino, dated March 2, 1947
Mourners march down the 700 block of West North Avenue.

Right: Lamplighter. 1947
Last vestiges of a world now unknown.

CRISSCROSSING THE NATION

TOP: RONALD REAGAN AND WIFE, JANE WYMAN, ARRIVE AT DEARBORN STATION ON OCTOBER 6, 1946. ABOVE:
JIMMY STEWART AND "NEWLY ACQUIRED" BRIDE, GLORIA, AT MUNICIPAL AIRPORT AUGUST 13, 1949. (PHOTO BY
DAVE MANN.) LEFT: CLARK GABLE AT POLK STREET STATION JUNE 15, 1946. (PHOTO BY LEONARD BASS.)

STARLIGHT EXPRESS
A "MANNISH" KATHARINE HEPBURN ARRIVES AT DEARBORN STATION MAY 17, 1948. (PHOTO BY LOUIS OKMIN.) LEFT: HUMPHREY BOGART AND HIS WIFE, LAUREN BACALL, ATTEND A WAR RALLY AT SOLDIER FIELD ON MAY 20, 1945. (PHOTO BY DAVE MANN.)

So natural. Photo by John Arabinko

Ruth Ann Steinhagen (left) faces major leaguer Eddie Waitkus (center) in Felony Court. "I'm scared and excited," she said. Right: Steinhagen in Cook County Jail on June 16, 1949, after she shot Waitkus in the chest at the Edgewater Beach Hotel. She was found legally insane and was committed to a mental institution. The incident inspired Bernard Malamud's novel "The Natural."

THE FIFTIES

Ralph Arvidson covered the saddest and most joyous events of the 1950s.

He was called to drive west on Lawrence Avenue in 1955 to photograph the bodies of three boys—John and Anton Schuessler and Robert Peterson—discovered in a forest preserve.

"I had never seen a sight like that before," he said. "You had three young boys lying there, not side by side but like somebody placed them there. It was gruesome, but I got over it."

The joyous moment—although short—came four years later when the White Sox took on the Los Angeles Dodgers in the World Series. "There was a sense of celebration because no Chicago team had made it to the series in 14 years," Arvidson said. "The Sox won the first game, but then things just fell apart."

Arvidson took up photography when he got a job working for the Associated Press while still in high school. "I told my mom, I loved being downtown," he said. From there, he moved to the *Sun-Times* darkroom and to the street. He retired to Arizona. He lived there one year and 22 days, but returned to Chicago.

"I didn't care for it too much," he said.

Patrons at Chester's Tavern in suburban Argo hail their hometown heroes on October 2, 1959. Photo by Doc Stryganek.

LULLABY OF THE LOOP. PHOTOS BY JOE KORDICK, 1950

ESSAY ON WORKERS AFTER MIDNIGHT. TRAVELING LOCKSMITH JAMES C. BRALY REPAIRS THE LATCH OF A PARKED
CAR AT LAKE STREET AND WACKER DRIVE ON MARCH 9. TOP RIGHT: CHARLES DAVIS CHANGES A MOVIE MARQUEE
AT THE ASTOR THEATER MARCH 15. RIGHT: FLORENCE WALTER CONTEMPLATES ART AND WORK AS SHE MOPS THE
ART INSTITUTE MARCH 10.

CHICAGO'S CASTLE IS RAZED. PHOTO BY EMMET BARDEN, FEBRUARY 2, 1950

THE MANSION OF POTTER AND BERTHA HONORE PALMER, BUILT FOR $1 MILLION IN 1882, IS TORN DOWN TO MAKE WAY FOR TWIN SKYSCRAPERS AT 1350 NORTH LAKE SHORE DRIVE.

Home for the holidays. Photo by Bill Sturm, December 23, 1950
Servicemen head through Union Station on their Christmas furloughs.

CTA's deadliest accident. 1950

A priest administers last rites to a victim of the Green Hornet streetcar disaster, which killed 33 people on May 25. The streetcar struck a gasoline truck near 62nd Place and State Street. Most of the victims were incinerated as they attempted to open the streetcar doors. Up to 15,000 viewed the site that night.

Top right: Remains of the streetcar. Right: Robert Mitchell, a relative of a rider, faints at the June 1 inquest.

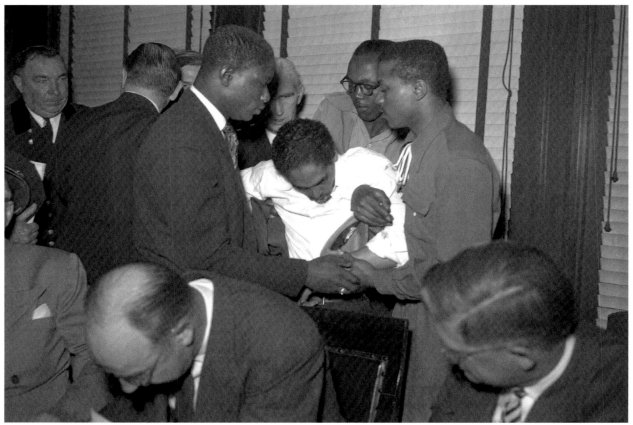

New model. Photo by Ralph Walters, February 18, 1951
Roberta Richards poses for amateur photographers at the Ford exhibit during the 1951 Automobile Show at the International Amphitheater.

Heading west. Photo by William DeLuga, June 29, 1951
Right: The route of the Congress Expressway is cleared. This photo was taken from the Main Post Office looking west. It was Chicago's first superhighway and was later renamed the Eisenhower Expressway.

THAT SUMMER FEELING. MAY 14, 1952

COMISKEY PARK GRANDSTANDS FILL AS THE WHITE SOX PREPARE TO TAKE THE FIELD IN SEASON'S FIRST NIGHT GAME.

FIREBALLER. PHOTO BY CHARLES GEKLER, JULY 31, 1955
PITCHING LEGEND SATCHEL PAIGE DEMONSTRATES HIS GRIP PRIOR TO THE NEGRO LEAGUE ALL-STAR GAME IN
COMISKEY PARK. HE WAS CALLED THE "BEST AND FASTEST PITCHER" BY JOE DIMAGGIO.

WE LIKE IKE. JULY 1952
GENERAL DWIGHT D. EISENHOWER TOURS CHICAGO DURING THE REPUBLICAN NATIONAL CONVENTION. HE DEFEATED SENATOR ROBERT TAFT TO WIN THE NOMINATION AT THE CONVENTION.

LEFT: A PERCH ABOVE THE CITY. PHOTO BY BILL STURM, OCTOBER 20, 1954
WALTER "WHITEY" SYFCZAK WORKS ON A FLAGPOLE ATOP THE CHICAGO TIMES BUILDING AT WACKER DRIVE AND FRANKLIN STREET.

BRONZEVILLE'S BEST. PHOTO BY CARMEN REPORTO, AUGUST 8, 1953
THE BUD BILLIKEN PARADE, ONE OF OLDEST AND LARGEST IN CHICAGO, WINDS THROUGH THE SOUTH SIDE.

RIGHT: A LITTLE HORSEPLAY. PHOTO BY WILLIAM PAUER, NOVEMBER 17, 1950
DEAN MARTIN AND JERRY LEWIS (TOP) JOIN ROLLER DERBY GIRLS BACKSTAGE AT THE CHICAGO THEATER.

BIG MAN ON BEACH. PHOTO BY CARMEN REPORTO, JUNE 25, 1954
FOREMAN HIGH SCHOOL GIRLS PLAY UP TO NEW LIFEGUARD JOSEPH DEL MONACO AT THE NORTH AVENUE BEACH.

THE LONG DRIVE HOME. PHOTO BY BILL KNEFEL, 1956

MOTORISTS SLOWLY MAKE THEIR WAY THROUGH A BLIZZARD ON NORTH LAKE SHORE DRIVE.

A MEMENTO OF WAR. PHOTO BY DAVE MANN, JUNE 1954
FLYING THE NAZI FLAG, THE CAPTURED U-505 PASSES THE WILSON AVENUE SHORELINE AS IT IS TOWED TO THE
MUSEUM OF SCIENCE AND INDUSTRY.

Cold War vigilance. Photo by Mel Larson, December 10, 1954
An antiaircraft gun battalion mans battle stations. A home front guard, established in 1953,
consisted of guns and 20 Nike Missile batteries strung along the lake.

Paris in Chicago. Photos by Elliott Robinson, May 1954

When the Art Institute of Chicago opened a photo show of life in Paris by Robert Doisneau, Chicago photographer Elliott Robinson responded by seeking the essence of Paris in his hometown. Left page: A maker of artificial eyes on West Montrose Avenue. Top: Outdoor painters, near the Art Institute. Left: Lorraine Tesch strikes a Parisian pose.

NATIVE SON RETURNS. SEPTEMBER 1955
MAMIE BRADLEY, MOTHER OF 14-YEAR-OLD EMMETT TILL WHO WAS BLUDGEONED TO DEATH BECAUSE HE WHISTLED AT A
WHITE WOMAN IN MISSISSIPPI, WEEPS AS HIS CASKET ARRIVES AT THE ILLINOIS CENTRAL STATION ON SEPTEMBER 2. MRS.
BRADLEY DEMANDED THE PINE BOX BE OPENED. "LET THE PEOPLE COME AND SEE WHAT THEY DID TO MY BOY." (PHOTO BY
DAVE MANN.) RIGHT: MRS. BRADLEY VIEWS THE OPEN CASKET AT HIS FUNERAL SEPTEMBER 6. (PHOTO BY RALPH WALTERS.)

Schuessler-Peterson murder. Photo by Dave Mann, October 22, 1955
Eleanor Schuessler is carried alongside caskets of her two young sons after collapsing near St. Tarcissus Roman Catholic Church. The boys, John and Anton Jr., were murdered with Robert Peterson in Robinson Woods.

Left: Unsolved crime. Photo by Bob Kotalik
Loretta Grimes grieves for her teenage daughters, Barbara and Patricia Grimes, who failed to return to their South Side home on December 28, 1956. The girls were last seen when they went to the Brighton Theater to see Elvis Presley in "Love Me Tender" for the 11th time. Their bodies were found 25 days later in a rural area.

Screaming for their hound dog. Photo by Bud Daley

Elvis Presley fans make their feelings known on March 29, 1957, at the International Amphitheater.

Left: Elvis is surrounded by his fans on November 13, 1956, as he publicizes his film "Love Me Tender."

A TREE GROWS ON STATE STREET. PHOTO BY DAVE MANN, JANUARY 9, 1956
WILLIAM DAVIS SHOVELS FLORIDA SAND AROUND A PALM TREE PLANTED IN THE DEAD OF WINTER AT STATE AND
MADISON STREETS. MODEL GLORIA MIZE ADDED A TROPICAL TOUCH TO THE PUBLICITY STUNT BY WEARING
A 24-KARAT GOLD BATHING SUIT.

RIGHT: LATE FOR WORK. PHOTO BY DAVE MANN, APRIL 21, 1955
RICHARD J. DALEY ARRIVES AT CITY HALL ON HIS FIRST DAY IN OFFICE.

Chicago in silhouette. Photos by Howard Lyon, April 26, 1959

ESCAPING THE HEAT. PHOTO BY WILLIAM PAUER, MARCH 14, 1958
NATHAN LEOPOLD (LEFT), WHO SERVED 33 YEARS IN PRISON FOR THE THRILL KILLING OF BOBBY FRANKS, WAITS AT O'HARE AIRPORT TO LEAVE CHICAGO FOR GOOD. HE IS WITH HIS ATTORNEY, ELMER GERTZ (RIGHT), AND FRIEND RALPH NEWMAN.

RIGHT: 'NOT SO PRIM A DONNA.' PHOTO BY BUD DALEY, NOVEMBER 19, 1955
OPERA DIVA MARIA CALLAS HISSES AT FEDERAL MARSHAL STANLEY PRINGLE, WHO SERVED A SUMMONS TO HER FOLLOWING HER PERFORMANCE IN "MADAME BUTTERFLY" AT THE CIVIC OPERA HOUSE. CALLAS WAS SUED BY A MANAGEMENT FIRM.

LANDMARKS. MAY 18, 1957
FRANK LLOYD WRIGHT FIGHTS A PLAN TO DESTROY THE ROBIE HOUSE. "IT COULD ONLY HAPPEN IN AMERICA," HE SAID.

RIGHT: STACKER OF WORDS. PHOTO BY DAVE MANN, AUGUST 19, 1957
CARL SANDBURG STROLLS ALONG WACKER DRIVE IN SEARCH OF MATERIAL FOR A NEW POEM ABOUT CHICAGO.

DEDICATED STAR. MARCH 2, 1959
ELIZABETH TAYLOR ATTENDS THE DEDICATION OF THE GRAVE OF HER EX-HUSBAND, FILM PRODUCER MICHAEL TODD,
AT THE JEWISH WALDHEIM CEMETERIES. SHE WAS WITH HER PHYSICIAN, DR. REXFORD KENNAMER.

SO GRACEFUL. FEBRUARY 17, 1955
MOVIE STAR GRACE KELLY VISITS THE AMBASSADOR EAST HOTEL. SHE BECAME THE PRINCESS OF MONACO
THE FOLLOWING YEAR.

'LOOK WHO'S HERE.' PHOTOS BY EDWARD DELUGA, MARCH 17, 1959
MARILYN MONROE STRUTS INTO TOWN TO PROMOTE HER NEW FILM, "SOME LIKE IT HOT."

CALUMET CITY HUSTLE
STRIP TEASE DANCERS WORK THE FAR SOUTH SIDE STEEL MILL BARS ON JUNE 9, 1959, DESPITE VICE RAIDS.
(PHOTO BY WILLIAM PAUER.) RIGHT: STRIPPERS ALIGHT FROM A POLICE BUS AT COOK COUNTY JAIL FOLLOWING A
RAID ON MAY 28, 1959. (PHOTO BY MEL LARSON.)

Our Lady of the Angels funeral. Photo by Dave Mann, December 5, 1958
Twenty-seven victims of the Our Lady of the Angels school fire are lined up before a temporary altar at the Northwest Armory, Kedzie and North avenues. Forty-five separate funerals were held that day for other victims.

Left: 'Teacher died with her pupils.' Photo by Bob Kotalik, December 3, 1958
A nun is carried down a ladder at the Our Lady of the Angels fire. Ninety-two students and three nuns died.

'Booing the Yanks.' Photo by Dave Mann, June 28, 1959
Bob Brockman cheers his White Sox to an American League pennant.

DRESSED FOR SUCCESS. PHOTO BY RALPH ARVIDSON, OCTOBER 8, 1959
NADINE ROJAS SHOWS OFF HER DRESS DECORATED WITH THE NAMES OF HER FAVORITE SOX PLAYERS.

Comiskey memories. Photo by Gene Pesek, April 6, 1960
With the World Series teams still on the board, steelworkers erect a new $300,000 scoreboard.

Left: 'Beer bath.' Photo by Charles Gekler, October 2, 1959
White Sox outfielder Al Smith backs up to Comiskey Park's left field wall in pursuit of a Charlie Neal home run in Game 2 of the 1959 World Series—and got soaked. For the rest of his life, Smith would brag he was the only player who ever drank a beer on the field during a Series game. (These photos were taken by a specially built action camera.)

THE SIXTIES

"EVERYTHING CHANGED IN THE SIXTIES," SAID GENE PESEK. "IT WAS A TRAUMATIC TIME. THE CITY STARTED TO CHANGE AND OUR CULTURE STARTED TO CHANGE. LIKE NOW, IT WAS A TIME WHEN EVERYTHING GOES."

PESEK PHOTOGRAPHED THE BEATLES WHEN THEY FIRST CAME TO CHICAGO (HE WORE EARPLUGS) AND WAS THERE WHEN THE BODIES OF EIGHT STUDENT NURSES WERE CARRIED OUT OF A BLOODY TOWNHOUSE ON 100TH STREET.

THE *SUN-TIMES* PHOTO STAFF TRANSFORMED, TOO, AS THE 35-MILLIMETER CAMERA WAS INTRODUCED AND A NEW CROWD OF YOUNG PHOTOGRAPHERS JOINED THE STAFF.

"THEY WERE A LITTLE PUSHY IN SOME RESPECTS," SAID PESEK. "BUT THEY WERE TAMED IN A SHORT WHILE. THEY LEARNED FROM US.

"THERE WERE SO MANY TRICKS IN OUR BUSINESS. WE KNEW HOW TO GET INTO PLACES AND WHO TO SEE. EVENTUALLY THEY LISTENED."

UNTIL THE MID-SIXTIES, PESEK FELT COMFORTABLE IN JUST ABOUT EVERY PART OF THE CITY. CIVIL RIGHTS RIOTS THAT ERUPTED IN WHITE AND BLACK NEIGHBORHOODS CHANGED THAT. "ALL OF A SUDDEN, YOU HAD TO BE CAREFUL WHEREVER YOU WENT," HE SAID.

"THE DESK WOULD TELL US TO GET A CUP OF COFFEE, BUT IT WASN'T SO EASY. THEY DIDN'T REALIZE THERE WAS OFTEN NO PLACE TO STOP."

THE FRONT DESK OF THE STARR HOTEL, WHERE MURDER SUSPECT RICHARD SPECK WAS ARRESTED ON JULY 23, 1966. PHOTO BY LARRY NOCERINO.

First TV debates. September 26, 1960

Left: Senator John F. Kennedy and Vice President Richard M. Nixon prepare to debate in Studio One at WBBM-TV. (Photograph by Luther Joseph.) Above: Hoopla surrounding the event that helped Kennedy win the election.

RETURN OF THE DIVA. PHOTO BY MEL LARSON, FEBRUARY 19, 1960
JOSEPHINE BAKER MAKES UP BACKSTAGE FOR AN APPEARANCE AT SOUTH SIDE'S REGAL THEATER.

LEFT: RING-A-DING DING. PHOTO BY LOUIS GIAMPA, MARCH 29, 1960
FRANK SINATRA ARRIVES AT THE ILLINOIS CENTRAL DEPOT ABOARD THE CITY OF MIAMI.

'GHOST TOWN.' PHOTO BY LARRY NOCERINO, MAY 12, 1962
THE ONCE-THRIVING UNION STOCKYARDS IS TORN DOWN. MOMENTS LATER, WORKMEN DYNAMITED THE CHIMNEY IN BACKGROUND. THE STOCKYARDS CLOSED IN 1971, AFTER MORE THAN A CENTURY.

SAVING THE CITY. PHOTO BY LARRY NOCERINO, JUNE 1, 1960
RICHARD NICKEL, ONE OF THE CITY'S FIRST ARCHITECTURAL PRESERVATIONISTS, SHOWS HIS PRIZE COLLECTION OF
LOUIS SULLIVAN ORNAMENT AT HIS SUBURBAN PARK RIDGE HOME.

'Lore and legend of Riverview.' Photos by Clarence Peters, dated November 5, 1967
Double exposures of rides to remember.

LEFT: SUMMERDALE POLICE TRIAL. PHOTO BY LOUIS GIAMPA, AUGUST 23, 1961
JUDGE JAMES B. PARSONS RESTS AFTER A JURY FOUND SEVEN SUMMERDALE DISTRICT POLICE OFFICERS GUILTY OF TAKING PART IN A NORTH SIDE BURGLARY RING. PARSONS DECIDED THEIR SENTENCE AND THE FATE OF ONE OTHER OFFICER WHO ASKED FOR A BENCH TRIAL.

TIGHTLIPPED. PHOTO BY JOE KORDICK, FEBRUARY 25, 1966
MUHAMMAD ALI, APPEARING BEFORE THE ILLINOIS ATHLETIC COMMISSION, REFUSES TO APOLOGIZE FOR "UNPATRIOTIC" REMARKS HE MADE EARLIER TO HIS KENTUCKY DRAFT BOARD. REFUSING TO FIGHT IN VIETNAM, ALI TOLD THE BOARD, "THOSE VIET CONGS ARE NOT ATTACKING ME."

STANLEY CUP CHAMPS. PHOTO BY MERRILL PALMER, APRIL 4, 1961
BLACKHAWKS BILL HAY (FROM LEFT), ERIC NESTERENKO AND BOBBY HULL RELAX IN DRESSING
ROOM AFTER STANLEY CUP VICTORY. THE HAWKS BEAT DETROIT RED WINGS 4 GAMES TO 2.

IN THE BEARS' DEN. NOVEMBER 17, 1963
WRIGLEY FIELD DURING BEARS-PACKERS GAME. THE BEARS WENT ON TO WIN THE NFL CHAMPIONSHIP AGAINST
THE NEW YORK GIANTS IN WRIGLEY FIELD 14-10.

THE MAN WHO SAID TOO MUCH. PHOTO BY BOB RUBEL, DECEMBER 5, 1962
COMEDIAN LENNY BRUCE IS ARRESTED FOR NIGHTCLUB OBSCENITY. HIS CONVICTION WAS LATER REVERSED.

On to the Hall of Fame. Photo by Bud Daley, June 15, 1964
Cubs outfielder Lou Brock posts a farewell note after his trade to the St. Louis Cardinals.

THE EARTH STOOD STILL. PHOTO BY BOB KOTALIK, NOVEMBER 25, 1963
PEOPLE WATCH THE FUNERAL OF JOHN F. KENNEDY AT THE ADMIRAL TV STORE ON MICHIGAN AVENUE.

MEET THE BEATLES. PHOTO BY GENE PESEK, SEPTEMBER 5, 1964
JOHN LENNON (FROM LEFT), GEORGE HARRISON AND PAUL MCCARTNEY ATTEND A PRESS CONFERENCE AT THE
STOCK YARD INN. IT WAS THE FIRST OF THREE CHICAGO PERFORMANCES.

THE FOUR WERE FAB. PHOTOS BY CLARENCE PETERS, AUGUST 12, 1966
THE BEATLES PLAY AT THE INTERNATIONAL AMPHITHEATER.

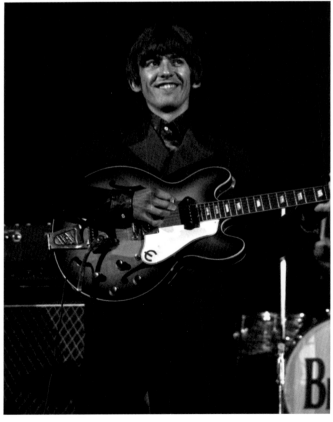

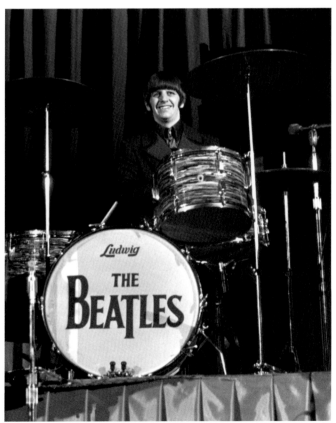

JUMP! PHOTO BY MICKEY RITO, AUGUST 30, 1964
ONLOOKERS WATCH A MAN ON A LEDGE NEAR THE TOP OF THE MORRISON HOTEL THREATEN TO JUMP. "THEY WERE
DISAPPOINTED," WROTE THE PHOTOGRAPHER. "HE SURRENDERED TO THE POLICE."

BLUE LAWS. PHOTO BY JOE MARINO, APRIL 28, 1964

FEMALE IMPERSONATORS, WHO WORK AS STRIPPERS, ARE ARRESTED IN A RAID AT THE NIGHT LIFE CLUB.

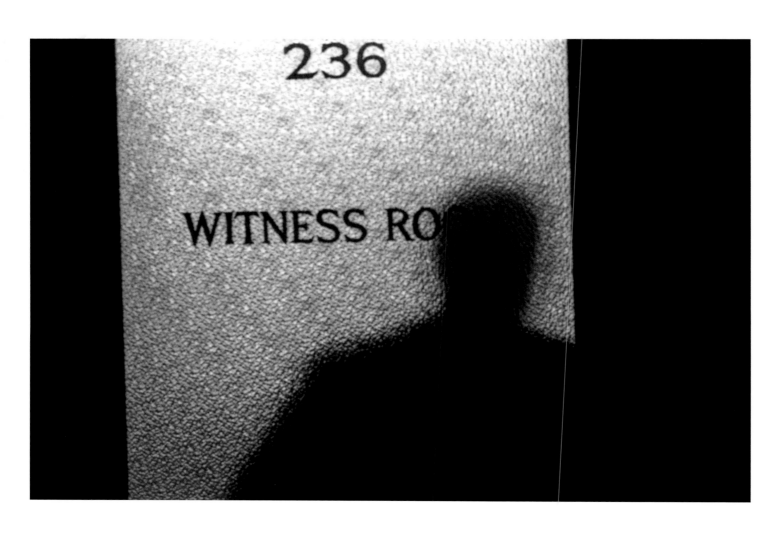

'U.S. vs. "Mr. Teamster."' Photo by Gene Pesek, May 20, 1964
Union boss Jimmy Hoffa meets with lawyers during his trial at the old Federal Courthouse.

They help cool gang violence. Dated December 11, 1965

Street workers take their message to gangs. Turf wars had lessened by the mid-1960s.

WHITE FIGHT. PHOTO BY MICKEY RITO, JULY 25, 1965
ANTI-INTEGRATIONISTS PICKET IN WINNETKA PRIOR TO THE ARRIVAL OF THE REVEREND MARTIN LUTHER KING JR.

LEFT: A LONG, HARD NIGHT. DATED AUGUST 13, 1965
PATROLMAN NEAL LOGUE IS BATTERED AFTER TRYING TO PUT DOWN WEST GARFIELD PARK RIOTING. SIXTY-TWO
PEOPLE WERE INJURED.

'MUTE DISBELIEF.' PHOTO BY GENE PESEK, JULY 14, 1966
ONLOOKERS WATCH AS POLICE REMOVE EIGHT STUDENT NURSES SLAIN AT 2319 E. 100TH STREET. RICHARD
SPECK LATER SAID HE KILLED THE NURSES BECAUSE IT "JUST WASN'T THEIR NIGHT."

BORN TO RAISE HELL. JULY 1966

RICHARD SPECK AT COOK COUNTY JAIL HOSPITAL. SPECK WAS ARRESTED AFTER HE TRIED TO COMMIT SUICIDE JULY 16 AT THE STARR HOTEL. HE WAS CONVICTED OF THE MURDERS IN 1967 AND DIED IN PRISON IN 1991.

KENNEDY MANIA. PHOTO BY JACK DYKINGA, OCTOBER 15, 1966
SENATOR ROBERT F. KENNEDY GREETS A CROWD AT RANDHURST SHOPPING CENTER.

RIGHT: UNCIVIL WRONGS. PHOTO BY LARRY NOCERINO, AUGUST 5, 1966
THE REVEREND MARTIN LUTHER KING JR. FALLS AFTER BEING STRUCK BY A ROCK FROM A TAUNTING MOB IN
MARQUETTE PARK. KING SAID HE NEVER MET "SUCH HOSTILITY, SUCH HATE, ANYWHERE IN MY LIFE."

RECORD SNOWSTORM. PHOTO BY BOB KOTALIK, AFTER JANUARY 26, 1967
GREENVIEW AVENUE IN ROGERS PARK FOLLOWING CITY'S 23-INCH BLIZZARD.

LEFT: MCCORMICK PLACE SKELETON. PHOTO BY HENRY HERR GILL, JANUARY 16, 1967
OFFICIALS MEET THE DAY AFTER FIRE DESTROYED THE MCCORMICK PLACE EXHIBITION HALL.

KING ASSASSINATION RIOTS. PHOTO BY DUANE HALL, APRIL 6, 1968
A NATIONAL GUARDSMAN AIMS HIS RIFLE ON WEST MADISON STREET DURING RIOTS FOLLOWING THE MEMPHIS
ASSASSINATION OF THE REVEREND MARTIN LUTHER KING JR.

LEFT: THE WEST SIDE IS BURNING. PHOTO BY BOB KOTALIK, APRIL 7, 1968
A HELICOPTER PASSES OVER BURNING WEST MADISON STREET. THIS PHOTO LOOKS EAST TOWARD THE LOOP.

A STRANGE, NEW WORLD
LOOTERS FLEE A STORE AT MADISON STREET AND LEAVITT AVENUE ON APRIL 5, 1968. (PHOTOS BY LARRY
NOCERINO.) RIGHT: A YOUNGSTER WATCHES A FIRE BURN ACROSS THE STREET AS U.S. ARMY TROOPERS MARCH
PAST ON APRIL 8, 1968. (PHOTO BY PERRY C. RIDDLE.)

And now, Bobby. Photo by Clarence Peters, June 6, 1968
Chicagoans congregate at State and Randolph streets to gather information on the electric news flasher about the assassination of Senator Robert F. Kennedy.

UP IN SMOKE. PHOTO BY JACK DYKINGA, MAY 5, 1967

DENNIS RIORDAN (FROM LEFT), IRWIN FELDMAN AND DON TYLKE BURN THEIR DRAFT CARDS AT THE WHEATON SELECTIVE SERVICE HEADQUARTERS.

SIGN LANGUAGE. PHOTO BY DUANE HALL, AUGUST 1968
A DEMONSTRATOR AT THE DEMOCRATIC NATIONAL CONVENTION FIGHTS OFF TEAR GAS AS HE WALKS IN FRONT OF A POLICE BARRICADE AT THE CONRAD HILTON HOTEL.

THE WHOLE WORLD WAS WATCHING. AUGUST 1968
VIETNAM WAR PROTESTERS FLOCK AROUND THE LOGAN STATUE IN GRANT PARK ON AUGUST 27. (PHOTO BY GARY SETTLE.) TOP RIGHT: POLICE OFFICER SPRAYS MACE AT PHOTOGRAPHER PAUL SEQUEIRA, WHO WAS INJURED ON AUGUST 28. (PHOTO BY PAUL SEQUEIRA.) MIDDLE RIGHT: OTHER OFFICERS GRAB PROTESTERS. (PHOTO BY PAUL SEQUEIRA.) BOTTOM RIGHT: PROTESTERS BAIT GUARDSMEN WITH CHANTS OF *SEIG HEIL* AUGUST 29. (PHOTO BY PERRY C. RIDDLE.)

The battle of Michigan Avenue. Photo by Charles Krejcsi, August 28, 1968
Illinois National Guardsmen stand guard in front of the Conrad Hilton Hotel.

"Gestapo tactics." Photo by Gary Settle, August 28, 1968

Mayor Richard J. Daley and son Richard M. Daley jeer Sen. Abraham Ribicoff at the Democratic National Convention as he criticizes Chicago "gestapo" tactics.

RIVERVIEW NO MORE. PHOTO BY JOE KORDICK, FEBRUARY 26, 1968
ALADDIN AND HIS CASTLE LOOK OVER THE WRECKAGE OF THE PAIR-O-CHUTES DURING THE PARK'S DEMOLITION.

End of a grande dame. Photo by Ralph Arvidson, December 23, 1967
Mike Enstock moves furniture from the North Side's pink landmark.

A SEA OF TRANQUILLITY. AUGUST 13, 1969
MOON MEN NEIL ARMSTRONG (FOREGROUND), MICHAEL COLLINS (RIGHT), AND EDWIN "BUZZ" ALDRIN JR. ARE
HONORED AT LA SALLE AND JACKSON STREETS. (PHOTO BY PERRY C. RIDDLE.) LEFT: THEIR TICKER TAPE PARADE
HEADED DOWN LA SALLE STREET. (PHOTO BY BILL MARES.)

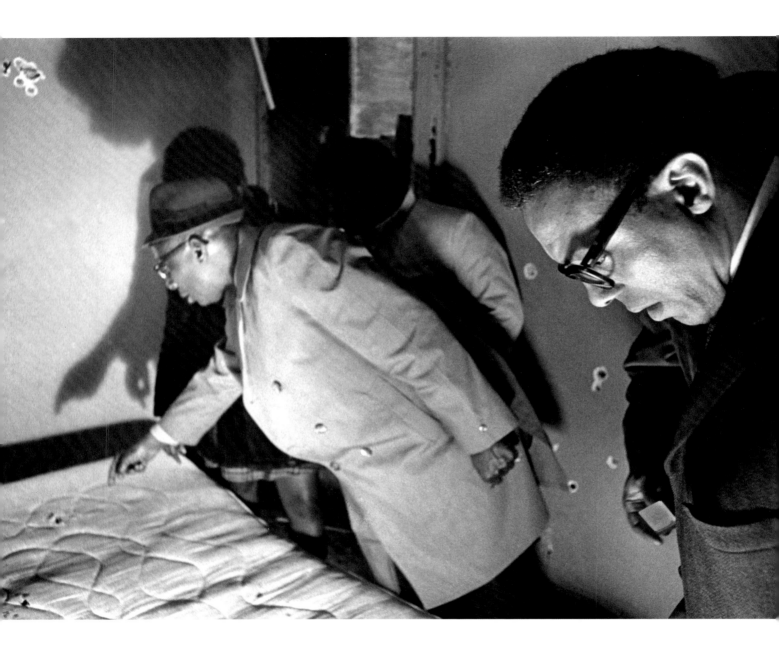

WHERE BLACK PANTHERS DIED. PHOTO BY JOHN H. WHITE, DECEMBER 5, 1969
STATE SENATORS CHARLES CHEW (LEFT) AND RICHARD NEWHOUSE INSPECT THE BED AND BULLET HOLES WHERE
BLACK PANTHERS LEADERS FRED HAMPTON AND MARK CLARK WERE SHOT BY POLICE THE PREVIOUS MORNING.

RIGHT: BOBBY RUSH SURRENDERS. PHOTO BY LARRY GRAFF, DECEMBER 6, 1969
BLACK PANTHERS SPOKESMAN BOBBY RUSH (SECOND FROM RIGHT) SURRENDERS TO RENAULT ROBINSON (RIGHT),
PRESIDENT OF AFRO-AMERICAN PATROLMAN'S LEAGUE, FOLLOWING THE FRED HAMPTON SHOOTING. HE WAS JOINED
BY HAMPTON'S BROTHER, WILLIAM (LEFT), AND THE REVEREND JESSE JACKSON.

THE SEVENTIES

BOB BLACK WAS THE *SUN-TIMES'* FIRST AFRICAN-AMERICAN PHOTOGRAPHER. HE LEARNED PHOTOGRAPHY FROM A CHURCH CAMERA CLUB. HE WAS HIRED BY THE *CHICAGO DEFENDER* IN 1965 AND STARTED WORK AT THE *SUN-TIMES* IN 1968.

"THE SEVENTIES WAS A TUMULTUOUS TIME," BLACK SAID. "THERE WAS LOTS OF TENSION AS THE CIVIL RIGHTS MOVEMENT WAS REACHING ITS APEX. THE POLITICAL STRUCTURE HAD TURNED A BLIND EYE ON THE BLACK COMMUNITY. THE HOUSING SITUATION HAD GOTTEN BAD, AND GANGS STARTED TO TAKE OFF. AND THERE WAS A REAL TRANSITION WHEN MAYOR DALEY DIED. CITY HALL JUST WENT UP FOR GRABS."

BLACK SAID HE WAS HIRED IN PART BECAUSE CIVIL RIGHTS ORGANIZATIONS PUT PRESSURE ON THE OWNERS OF NEWSPAPERS TO BETTER UNDERSTAND THE AFRICAN-AMERICAN COMMUNITY.

BLACK FELT OBSTACLES, PARTICULARLY FROM EDITORS UNWILLING TO GIVE HIM PRIME ASSIGNMENTS. "THOSE BARRIERS WERE NOT OVERT," HE SAID. "IT WAS AN ATTITUDINAL THING THAT YOU COULD FEEL."

THE *SUN-TIMES*, BLACK SAID, HAD ACTIVIST STAFF MEMBERS WHO WERE COMMITTED TO USING THE CAMERA TO RIGHT SOCIAL WRONG DURING THE SIXTIES. HE FOLLOWED THEIR LEAD.

"I WAS DETERMINED TO USE MY ACTIVISM TO TELL STORIES FROM THE BLACK COMMUNITY THAT WERE DIFFERENT FROM WHAT WHITE PEOPLE WERE USED TO SEEING."

A VENDOR SPREADS THE NEWS THAT PRESIDENT NIXON WILL STEP DOWN FROM OFFICE ON AUGUST 9, 1974.
PHOTO © JOHN H. WHITE

THE GENERATION GAP. PHOTO BY PAUL SEQUEIRA, MAY 9, 1970

RIGHT: PROM PARTY. PHOTO BY DON BIERMAN, JUNE 20, 1970
TONY KOSTOGIANNES AND ILENE ZHOWICZ POSE FOR PICTURES AT A VON STEUBEN HIGH SCHOOL PRE-PROM
GET-TOGETHER AT THE HOLLYWOOD PARK TENNIS COURT.

FRIENDS IN DEED. PHOTO BY CHARLES KREJCSI, SEPTEMBER 28, 1971
CRIME SYNDICATE LEADERS TONY ACCARDO (LEFT) AND JOSEPH "JOEY THE DOVES" AIUPPA WATCH A HEARSE
CARRYING GANGLAND BOSS FELIX "MILWAUKEE PHIL" ALDERISIO TO HIS GRAVE AT QUEEN OF HEAVEN MAUSOLEUM
IN SUBURBAN HILLSIDE.

RIGHT: LONGEST TRIAL. PHOTO BY FRED STEIN, JULY 10, 1972
COOK COUNTY STATE'S ATTORNEY EDWARD V. HANRAHAN (RIGHT BACKGROUND) DISCUSSES LEGAL STRATEGY
DURING A VISIT TO THE APARTMENT WHERE BLACK PANTHER LEADERS WERE SLAIN IN 1969. HANRAHAN WAS A
DEFENDANT IN A FEDERAL CIVIL LAWSUIT THAT DRAGGED ON FOR 12 YEARS.

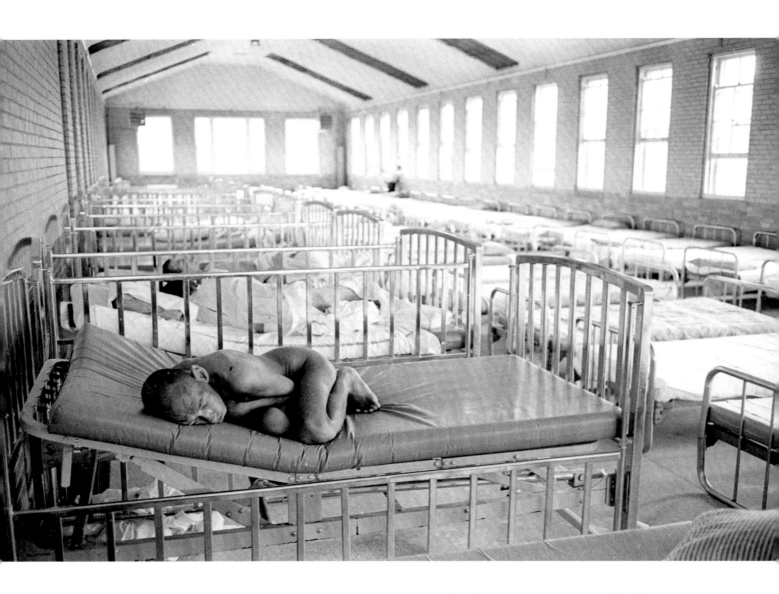

JACK DYKINGA BECAME THE FIRST *SUN-TIMES*
PHOTOGRAPHER TO WIN THE PULITZER PRIZE, HONORED FOR A
SERIES OF PHOTOGRAPHS TAKEN IN APRIL AND JULY 1970 AT THE
STATE SCHOOLS FOR THE MENTALLY RETARDED IN DOWNSTATE
DIXON AND LINCOLN.

DYKINGA SPENT THREE DAYS AT THE SCHOOLS. "IT WAS A
REAL SHOCK TO MY SENSES, LIKE NOTHING I HAD EVER SEEN
BEFORE," HE LATER SAID. "FOR THE FIRST HOUR AND A HALF, I
DIDN'T TAKE ANY PICTURES AT ALL. I JUST WATCHED AND WAS
OVERCOME BY HORROR."

DYKINGA SAID HE WAS RUSHED. "WE WENT FROM COTTAGE TO
COTTAGE, AND I THINK SOME OF THE PATIENTS THERE REACTED
THE WAY SMALL CHILDREN REACT. THEY WERE CURIOUS, YOU
KNOW, AND THEY WOULD REACH OUT AND TOUCH THE CAMERA."

AFTER THE PHOTOGRAPHS WERE PUBLISHED, STATE
OFFICIALS CURTAILED PLANS TO REDUCE FUNDING TO THE
DEPARTMENT OF MENTAL HEALTH.

JACK DYKINGA'S 1971 PULITZER PRIZE PORTFOLIO IN FEATURE PHOTOGRAPHY

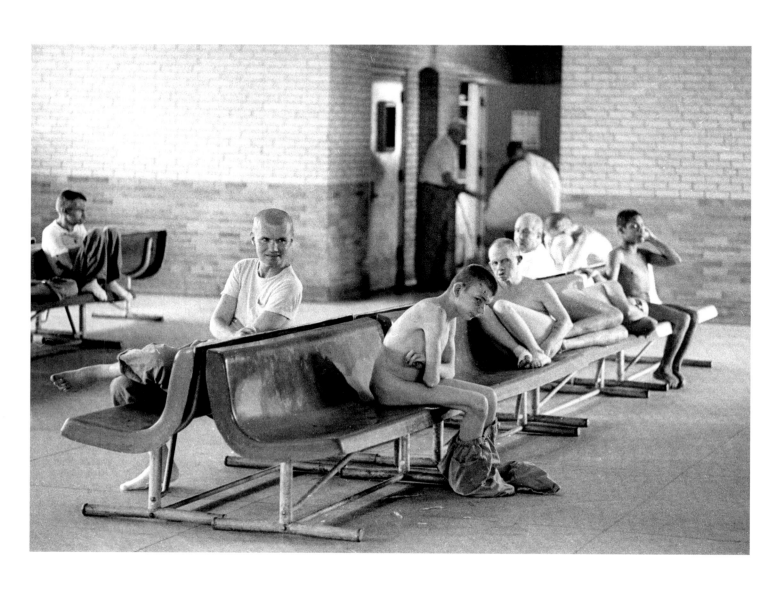

JACK DYKINGA'S 1971 PULITZER PRIZE PORTFOLIO IN FEATURE PHOTOGRAPHY

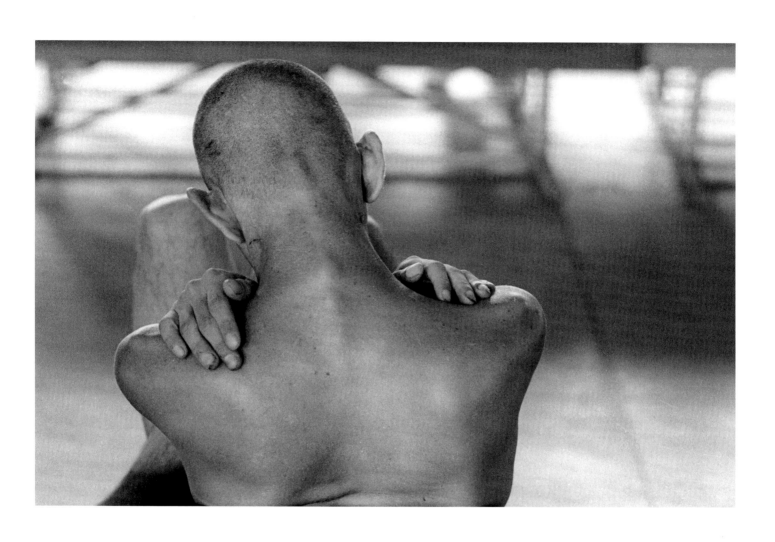

WHO'S ON STAGE? PHOTO BY BOB BLACK, AUGUST 17, 1971
PETE TOWNSHEND AND THE WHO PERFORM AT THE AUDITORIUM THEATRE.

RIGHT: BRING BACK THE BLUES. PHOTO BY BOB BLACK, JUNE 1, 1971
MUDDY WATERS PLAYS AT MR. KELLY'S NIGHTCLUB, WHERE HE RECORDED AN ALBUM.

CRUSHED. OCTOBER 30, 1972
FORTY-FIVE PASSENGERS ON AN ILLINOIS CENTRAL COMMUTER TRAIN WERE KILLED AND 332 INJURED WHEN THE
TRAIN BACKED INTO THE 27TH STREET STATION AND COLLIDED WITH ANOTHER TRAIN.

It fell from the sky. Photo by Edmund Jarecki, December 9, 1972
The tail fin of a United Airlines 737 remains intact after the plane crashed into homes on the
Southwest Side. Forty-three passengers and two people on the ground were killed.

NIXON'S THE ONE. PHOTO BY M. LEON LOPEZ, MARCH 14, 1974
DEMONSTRATORS REFLECT THE SPLIT IN THE NATION OVER PRESIDENT RICHARD NIXON, WHO WAS VISITING THE CITY.

LEFT: THE MOUTH THAT ROARED. PHOTO BY JACK LENAHAN, MARCH 19, 1970
U.S. ATTORNEY GENERAL JOHN N. MITCHELL AND HIS WIFE, MARTHA, ATTEND A POLITICAL RECEPTION.

TEARS FOR THE MESSENGER. PHOTO BY HOWARD SIMMONS, FEBRUARY 26, 1975
MINISTER LOUIS FARRAKHAN EULOGIZES THE LATE ELIJAH MUHAMMAD AT MEMORIAL SERVICE.

LEFT: *ALAIKUM-SALAAM.* © JOHN H. WHITE, FEBRUARY 26, 1974
BLACK MUSLIMS JOIN IN GREETINGS AT SAVIOURS' DAY ON THE SOUTH SIDE.

KODAK SAFETY
KODAK TRI X PAN FILM
KODAK SAFETY FILM
KODAK TRI X PAN FILM
KODAK SAFETY FILM
3
5
6
10
11
11A
12
12A
18
18A
19

BUNNIES FROM HEAVEN. PHOTO BY JOHN H. WHITE, MARCH 1, 1973
PLAYBOY BUNNY JUDY KUCIC SCREAMS AFTER BEING CHOSEN CHICAGO "BUNNY OF THE YEAR" AT THE PLAYBOY CLUB.

LEFT: THE KING IS BACK. PHOTO BY JACK LENAHAN, JUNE 17, 1972
PHOTO CONTACT SHEET SHOWS SHOTS FROM ELVIS PRESLEY'S CONCERT AT CHICAGO STADIUM.

His 500th homer. Photo by Henry Herr Gill, May 12, 1970
"I feel like I'm 12 years old," Ernie Banks told a reporter.

Right: What was he thinking? Photo by Randy Leffingwell, March 1, 1976
Sox owner Bill Veeck displays new team uniforms, modeled by former players Moose Skowron (from
left), Moe Drabowsky, Jim Rivera and Dave Nicholson.

Help for his father. Photo by Perry C. Riddle, December 20, 1976
Richard M. Daley signals to paramedics as he rushes his stricken father to the hospital. Mayor
Richard J. Daley died of a heart attack at age 74 after a visit to his doctor.

Right: Last ride through Bridgeport. Photo by Fred Stein, December 23, 1976
Funeral cortege leaves Nativity of Our Lord Church in Bridgeport and carries the mayor's body past
his home on South Lowe Avenue.

New man from Bridgeport. Photo by Richard Derk, October 17, 1977

Mayor Michael A. Bilandic speaks at ceremonies rededicating the Chicago Public Library as the
Chicago Cultural Center. Seated are Richard M. Daley (left) and Bilandic's wife, Heather.

The *Chicago Sun-Times* purchased and operated a North Side tavern called the Mirage for four months in an effort to uncover and document rumored shakedowns of tavern owners.

As reporters chronicled their daily conversations with city officials, photographers Jim Frost and Gene Pesek recorded the action from a concealed loft overlooking the tavern. They turned up the jukebox so nobody could hear the click of the shutter.

Left: A fire inspector takes a payoff for overlooking code violations on July 27.

Above: A building inspector picks up an envelope containing $15 for overlooking code violations the following day.

The Mirage. Photos by Jim Frost, 1978

NEO-NAZIS CALL OFF MARCH. PHOTO BY JACK LENAHAN, JUNE 22, 1978
FRANK COLLIN CURTAILS HIS PLAN TO SEND DEMONSTRATORS INTO THE CHICAGO SUBURB OF SKOKIE.

SERIAL KILLER ARRESTED. PHOTO BY JERRY TOMASELLI, DECEMBER 22, 1978
JOHN WAYNE GACY, LATER CONVICTED OF MURDERING 33 YOUNG MEN, IS LED INTO THE DES PLAINES POLICE STATION.

TOPPLED FROM THE TRACKS. PHOTO BY CHUCK KIRMAN, FEBRUARY 4, 1977
TERRIFIED PASSENGERS FILL A CHICAGO EL TRAIN THAT HANGS AT WABASH AVENUE AND LAKE STREET DURING
EVENING RUSH HOUR. ELEVEN RIDERS WERE KILLED.

NATION'S WORST AIR CRASH. PHOTOS BY RANDY LEFFINGWELL, MAY 25, 1979
TOP: AFTER AMERICAN AIRLINES FLIGHT 191 CRASHED, THE ONLY JOB LEFT TO RESCUERS WAS TO MARK THE LOCATIONS
OF 273 BODIES. ABOVE: PARTS OF THE WRECKAGE FELL WITHIN FEET OF TRAILER VILLAGE NORTH OF O'HARE AIRPORT.

'TEARS FOR A BUDDY.' PHOTO BY JERRY TOMASELLI, AUGUST 13, 1979
A CONSTRUCTION WORKER GRIEVES FOR A FALLEN CO-WORKER AFTER THE ROOF OF THE ROSEMONT SPORTS ARENA
COLLAPSED. FIVE PEOPLE WERE KILLED IN THE CONSTRUCTION ACCIDENT.

A CLOUD OF DUST. PHOTO BY PERRY C. RIDDLE, JUNE 1, 1979
CLEMENTE HIGH SCHOOL SCORES THE WINNING RUN IN THE PUBLIC LEAGUE CHAMPIONSHIP GAME AS IT DEFEATS
KENNEDY HIGH SCHOOL.

IRISH EYES ARE SMILING. PHOTO BY KEVIN HORAN, MARCH 17, 1979
A ST. PATRICK'S DAY MARCHER WITH A MIRROR SHOWS PARADE WATCHERS HOW SILLY THEY LOOK AS HE WALKS
DOWN CLARK STREET.

THE NIGHT RECORDS RAINED. PHOTO BY CHUCK KIRMAN, JULY 12, 1979
A CAPACITY CROWD STORMS THE FIELD AT COMISKEY PARK ON DISCO DEMOLITION NIGHT. CHICAGO POLICE WERE
CALLED IN TO CLEAR THE FIELD.

FIGHTING JANE. DECEMBER 1979
CTA WORKERS GO ON STRIKE DURING THE HEIGHT OF THE CHRISTMAS SHOPPING SEASON AFTER MAYOR JANE
BYRNE CHALLENGED THE UNION. HERE SHE RIDES AN EL TRAIN IN THE LOOP AT THE EVENING RUSH HOUR ON
DECEMBER 18. (PHOTO BY HENRY HERR GILL.) LEFT: A FULL TRAIN PULLS AWAY FROM THE BELMONT STATION ON
DECEMBER 20. RIDERS CLUNG TO THE BACK OF THE TRAIN AND BETWEEN CARS. (PHOTO BY KEVIN HORAN.)

THE EIGHTIES

NANCY STUENKEL CAME TO THE
SUN-TIMES FROM A SUBURBAN PAPER.
THE SWITCH WAS DRAMATIC.

"I HAD A LOT TO LEARN IN TERMS
OF COVERING ASSIGNMENTS, SHE SAID.
"DOWNTOWN WE WERE DOING TWO OR
THREE ASSIGNMENTS A DAY, ROUTINELY
SHOOTING AND DEVELOPING HUNDREDS OF
PHOTOS A DAY. I WAS NOT ASSERTIVE ON
BREAKING NEWS WHEN I STARTED, BUT
SEVERAL STAFF MEMBERS TAUGHT ME
HOW TO PUSH AND SHOVE AND, WELL, BE
RELENTLESS."

THE *SUN-TIMES* WENT THROUGH
ITS GREATEST TRANSITION DURING THE
EIGHTIES AS THE PAPER WAS SOLD TWICE.
EACH NEW OWNER PUT A DIFFERENT
STAMP ON THE PAPER—TAKING IT
DOWNSCALE, UPSCALE AND FINALLY MID-
SCALE. PHOTOGRAPHERS WERE EXPECTED
TO CHANGE WITH THE PAPER'S NEW
PERSONA.

STUENKEL REMEMBERS THE
DECADE PHOTOGRAPHICALLY AS AN ERA
WHEN THE *SUN-TIMES* STAFF STARTED
SHOOTING COLOR FOR THE PAPER'S FRONT
AND BACK PAGES. THESE WERE
PARTICULARLY DIFFICULT YEARS AS
PHOTOGRAPHERS USED COLOR
TRANSPARENCY FILM, WHICH FORCED
THEM TO BE MUCH MORE PRECISE ON
EXPOSURE.

FOR MANY ON THE STAFF, THE
EIGHTIES WILL BE REMEMBERED AS THE
ERA OF HAROLD WASHINGTON, SHE SAID.
"HE WAS VIBRANT AND FUN, NOT AFRAID
OF A GOOD PHOTO OPPORTUNITY. HE
WALKED IN A ROOM AND THE ENERGY
LEVEL KICKED UP. HE COULD WEAR A
SOMBRERO, SLING A HUGE SALAMI ON HIS
SHOULDER, OR SIP SAKE.

"HE MADE IT EASY FOR US."

THE BRIGHT ONE: REPUTED GANGSTER
JOSEPH "JOEY THE CLOWN" LOMBARDO
USES THE PAPER TO HIDE HIS FACE AS HE
LEAVES COURT ON MARCH 11, 1981.
PHOTO BY PERRY C. RIDDLE.

EATING PRETTY. PHOTO BY PETE SOUZA, SEPTEMBER 26, 1982
POLICE OFFICERS JOHN DEMOS (FROM LEFT), JOHN BORATTO AND STEVE VILLARREAL GET A TASTE OF RIBS AT THE
FIRST MIKE ROYKO RIBFEST.

WELCOME TO THE 'HOOD.' PHOTO BY KEVIN HORAN, APRIL 3, 1987
MAYOR JANE BYRNE AND HER HUSBAND, JAY MCMULLEN, SHARE BREAKFAST AT THE CABRINI-GREEN HOUSING
PROJECT. THEY MOVED IN FOR FOUR WEEKS TO QUELL A GANG RIOT.

LITTLE WALTER. PHOTO BY RICHARD DERK, JULY 31, 1980
WALTER POLOVCHAK, 12, ENTERS COURTROOM WITH HIS LAWYERS. HE REFUSED TO RETURN TO THE SOVIET UNION
WITH HIS PARENTS BECAUSE HE LIKED AMERICAN LIFE. HE WAS ALLOWED TO STAY.

CHICAGO LOVES CHICAGO. PHOTO BY PHIL VELASQUEZ. AUGUST 14, 1983
CHICAGOFEST CROWD APPLAUDS DURING THE PERFORMANCE OF THE ROCK BAND CHICAGO AT SOLDIER FIELD.

WIND BLOWN. PHOTO BY DOM NAJOLIA, OCTOBER 20, 1982
PILOT ROBERT MENDEZ TAKES PHOTOGRAPHER FOR A SPIN ABOVE CHICAGO IN HIS EXPERIMENTAL PLANE.

LEFT: 'SPIDER' DAN. PHOTO BY RICHARD DERK, MAY 25, 1981
DANIEL GOODWIN CLIMBS PAST THE 83RD FLOOR ON HIS WAY TO THE TOP OF THE SEARS TOWER. GOODWIN, WHO USED
SUCTION CUPS, WAS ARRESTED WHEN HE MADE IT TO THE TOP. HE ALSO CLIMBED THE JOHN HANCOCK BUILDING.

A COLLECTION OF 20 PHOTOGRAPHS TAKEN BY JOHN
H. WHITE WON THE PULITZER PRIZE IN 1982.

AMONG THE WORK HE SUBMITTED WERE PHOTOS OF
BALLET STUDENTS AT A PRIVATE NORTH SIDE
PERFORMING ARTS ACADEMY, A WORKMAN AT THE FIELD
MUSEUM BRUSHING THE TEETH OF A 75-MILLION-YEAR-
OLD SKELETON AND PICTURES OF THE ROBERT TAYLOR
AND CABRINI-GREEN HOUSING PROJECTS.

HE WON, HE SAID, BECAUSE HE ALWAYS CARRIES A
CAMERA WITH HIM AND BECAUSE HE BLENDS INTO THE
LIFE AROUND HIM.

"AS I WALK DOWN THE STREET, I DON'T LOOK FOR
GOOD SHOTS," WHITE SAID. "I RECOGNIZE THEM. WHEN
YOU ARE IN TUNE WITH LIFE, YOU SEE THINGS."

THE DAY AFTER THE AWARD WAS ANNOUNCED,
WHITE CONFESSED THAT HE LONG HAD A DREAM OF
WINNING THE PULITZER.

"MY REAL GOAL HAS BEEN TO DO THE DAY'S JOB,"
HE SAID. "TO CAPTURE THE MOMENT THAT DEPICTS THE
STORY—THAT'S THE AWARD."

JOHN H. WHITE'S 1982 PULITZER PRIZE PORTFOLIO IN FEATURE PHOTOGRAPHY

John H. White's 1982 Pulitzer Prize Portfolio in Feature Photography

REMEMBERING CARDINAL CODY. PHOTO BY DOM NAJOLIA, MAY 1, 1982
A MOURNER VISITS THE CRYPT OF JOHN PATRICK CODY, ROMAN CATHOLIC ARCHBISHOP OF CHICAGO FROM 1965 UNTIL 1982, AT MOUNT CARMEL CEMETERY IN HILLSIDE.

RIGHT: LEADER OF HIS FLOCK. PHOTO BY RICHARD DERK, AUGUST 25, 1982
JOSEPH BERNARDIN IS INSTALLED AS ARCHBISHOP OF CHICAGO AT HOLY NAME CATHEDRAL.

'BEFORE IT'S TOO LATE.' PHOTO BY PHIL VELASQUEZ, MARCH 21, 1983
HAROLD WASHINGTON DEBATES REPUBLICAN CHALLENGER BERNARD EPTON. WASHINGTON WON THE ELECTION
APRIL 12, 1983.

Historic moment. Photo by Keith Hale, April 29, 1983

Cook County Circuit Judge Charles E. Freeman swears in Harold Washington as Chicago's 42nd mayor at Navy Pier on April 29, 1983. Outgoing Mayor Jane Byrne is at right.

A PRISONER NO MORE. PHOTO BY RICH HEIN, APRIL 4, 1985
GARY DOTSON LEAVES THE JOLIET CORRECTIONAL CENTER. DOTSON WAS CONVICTED OF RAPE, BUT HIS SENTENCE WAS COMMUTED WHEN HIS "VICTIM" RECANTED HER STORY. HIS CONVICTION WAS LATER OVERTURNED BASED ON DNA TESTS.

RIGHT: RETURN OF CHICAGO TWO. PHOTOS BY JACK LENAHAN, FEBRUARY 21, 1985
ABBIE HOFFMAN (ABOVE) AND JERRY RUBIN RETURN TO RECALL THEIR SIXTIES DAYS IN THE "CONSPIRACY EIGHT."

THEIR NEW NATION. PHOTO BY AL PODGORSKI, SEPTEMBER 9, 1984

A KOREAN PARADE WINDS DOWN LAWRENCE AVENUE IN THE ALBANY PARK NEIGHBORHOOD.

MEETING ON THE MOUND. PHOTO BY NANCY STUENKEL, JULY 27, 1984
CATCHER BOBBY RYAN CONFERS WITH PITCHER ROGER OWENS DURING THE SPECIAL OLYMPICS IN GRANT PARK.

SWEET AND PUNKY

CHICAGO BEARS' GREATEST RUNNING BACK, WALTER PAYTON, KNOWN AS "SWEETNESS," DURING THE CHAMPIONSHIP 1985-86 SEASON. (PHOTO BY JOHN H. WHITE.) LEFT: BEARS QUARTERBACK JIM MCMAHON, THE "PUNKY QB," AT THE START OF 1986 FOOTBALL PRACTICE IN PLATTEVILLE, WISCONSIN. (PHOTO BY PHIL VELASQUEZ.)

A WAR REMEMBERED. PHOTO BY AL PODGORSKI, JUNE 13, 1986
JANE RYAN CRIES AS SHE CHEERS THE VIETNAM VETERANS PARADE THROUGH THE LOOP. MORE THAN 1 MILLION
SPECTATORS CAME TO CHEER 250,000 FORMER SOLDIERS.

THE DALEY LEGACY. PHOTO BY AL PODGORSKI, FEBRUARY 20, 1986
RICHARD M. DALEY HOLDS HIS DAUGHTER ELIZABETH AS HIS FAMILY GATHERS TO REMEMBER HIS FATHER, THE
FORMER MAYOR RICHARD J. DALEY, A DECADE AFTER HIS DEATH.

MAYOR WASHINGTON'S SUDDEN DEATH. PHOTO BY AL PODGORSKI. NOVEMBER 25, 1987
CHICAGOANS GATHER AT THE DALEY CENTER PLAZA FOR A PRAYER VIGIL FOR THE LATE MAYOR HAROLD WASHINGTON.

LYING IN STATE. PHOTO BY AL
PODGORSKI, NOVEMBER 29, 1987
A STREAM OF MOURNERS FILL CITY
HALL THROUGH THE NIGHT TO VIEW
MAYOR WASHINGTON'S CASKET.

Night comes to Wrigley.
Cubs pitcher Al Nipper looks in vain for a break in the rain during the first night game at Wrigley Field on August 8, 1988. The game was canceled. (Photo by Tom Cruze.) Left: Workers install the first set of lights April 26, 1988. (Photo by Jim Klepitsch.)

EARLY MORNING BAPTISMS
CELEBRANTS EMERGE FROM LAKE MICHIGAN AT 31ST STREET ON AUGUST 7, 1989. (PHOTO BY JON SALL.) TOP: CHESTER BYRD CARRIES DEMETRA MCFALL TOWARD THE OPEN ARMS OF THE REV. PAUL SOUTHERLAND ON AUGUST 21, 1988. (PHOTO BY AMANDA ALCOCK.). LEFT: BYRD LEANS ON SOUTHERLAND AFTER HIS OWN RITUAL DUNKING. (PHOTO BY AMANDA ALCOCK.)

THE NINETIES . . .

PABLO MARTINEZ MONSIVAIS TRANSFORMED FROM A COLLEGE INTERN TO A *SUN-TIMES* PHOTOGRAPHER IN 13 WEEKS.

MONSIVAIS GREW UP IN THE LITTLE VILLAGE NEIGHBORHOOD ON THE SOUTHWEST SIDE. "WE TOOK THE *SUN-TIMES*, *TRIBUNE*, *DAILY NEWS*, WHOEVER MADE US THE BEST DEAL," HE SAID. "I GREW UP LOOKING AT PHOTOS OF THE REAGAN ASSASSINATION AND THE COLUMBIA DISASTER. PHOTOJOURNALISM WAS A RECORDER OF HISTORY, AND I WANTED TO BE PART OF IT."

MONSIVAIS WAS RAW AT THE START. SO RAW AND INEXPERIENCED, IN FACT, THAT HE LEFT HIS EQUIPMENT AT HIS FIRST ASSIGNMENT. IT TOOK HIM ALMOST THREE YEARS TO FEEL CONFIDENT. BUT HE BROUGHT WITH HIM A BASIC KNOWLEDGE OF COMPUTERS THAT HELPED THE *SUN-TIMES* SWITCH INTO A NEW TECHNOLOGICAL AGE.

"THE NINETIES WILL BE REMEMBERED FOR THE IMPLEMENTATION OF DIGITAL IMAGERY," HE SAID. "WE LEARNED BY TRIAL AND ERROR."

THE *SUN-TIMES* BOUGHT ITS FIRST DIGITAL CAMERAS AND SCANNERS IN THE EARLY 1990S, PRIMARILY TO MEET THE DEADLINE PRESSURE OF CHICAGO BULLS PLAYOFF GAMES AND FOR THE DEMOCRATIC NATIONAL CONVENTION IN 1996.

"I THOUGHT MY FIRST DIGITAL CAMERA WAS WONDERFUL, A NEW TOY, BUT IN RETROSPECT IT WAS JUNKY," HE SAID. "THE COLOR BALANCE WAS BAD, THE TIMING WAS OFF, AND THE BATTERIES DIDN'T LAST.

"BUT WE ALL KNEW IT WAS THE FUTURE."

TO TODAY

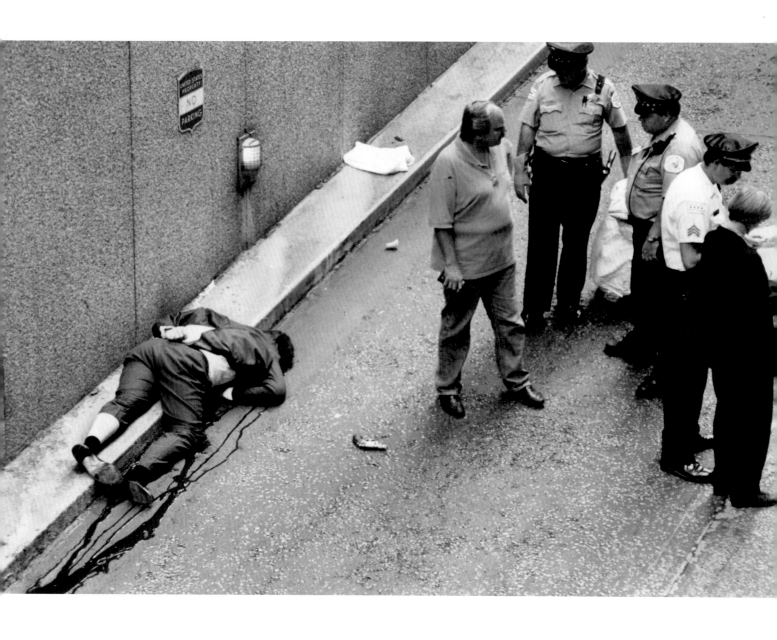

ESCAPE ATTEMPT. PHOTO BY BRIAN JACKSON, JULY 20, 1992
THE BODY OF ACCUSED BANK ROBBER JEFFREY ERICKSON LIES ON THE RAMP OF THE DIRKSEN FEDERAL BUILDING.
ERICKSON SHOT TWO GUARDS, THEN SHOT HIMSELF, SAYING, "I'M GOING TO DIE ANYWAY."

THE LURE OF GANGS. PHOTO BY RICH HEIN, MARCH 19, 1992
EVEN IN CUSTODY, TEENAGERS SHOW THEIR GANG TATTOOS AT THE COOK COUNTY JUVENILE TEMPORARY
DETENTION CENTER. THE 16-YEAR-OLD ON THE LEFT WAS HELD FOR ATTEMPTED MURDER OF A POLICE OFFICER.

BACK IN ORBIT. PHOTO BY JOHN H. WHITE, OCTOBER 15, 1992
DR. MAE JEMISON JOINS THE MORGAN PARK HIGH SCHOOL POMPON TEAM. ABOUT 8,000 STUDENTS HONORED THE
MORGAN PARK GRADUATE, WHO BECAME FIRST BLACK WOMAN TO TRAVEL IN SPACE.

IRON MIKE. PHOTO BY RICHARD A. CHAPMAN, JUNE 15, 1990
MIKE DITKA OFFERS ADVICE AND AN AUTOGRAPH TO BEARS FAN TODD GOLDMAN. DITKA PLAYED ON THE 1963
CHAMPIONSHIP BEARS AND COACHED THE TEAM FOR 11 YEARS.

DANTRELL DAVIS REMEMBERED. 1992.
HARVEY REYNOLDS (LEFT) AND MICHAEL REYNOLDS SIT IN THE WINDOW OF THEIR NINTH-FLOOR CABRINI-GREEN APARTMENT. THEY WERE BEST FRIENDS OF DANTRELL DAVIS, A 7-YEAR-OLD BOY KILLED BY A SNIPER AS HE WALKED TO SCHOOL. (PHOTO BY JOHN H. WHITE.) LEFT: RENISHA JAMES LIGHTS A CANDLE IN MEMORY OF DAVIS AT A VIGIL OCTOBER 24 AT THE FEDERAL BUILDING PLAZA. (PHOTO BY BOB BLACK.)

LEFT: PILEUP. PHOTO BY SCOTT STEWART, JANUARY 2, 1993
FORTY-CAR ACCIDENT ON THE KENNEDY EXPRESSWAY FROM AN ICE STORM THAT SWEPT THE CITY.

A LITTLE DIP. PHOTO BY JON SALL, AUGUST 24, 1994
TOW TRUCK OPERATOR DIVES TO EXAMINE OUT-OF-CONTROL CAR THAT ENDED UP IN A ROGERS PARK POOL.

FOX RIVER GROVE TRAGEDY. PHOTO BY RICHARD A. CHAPMAN.
KIMBERLY SCHNEIDER AGONIZES AS SHE AWAITS WORD ABOUT HER DAUGHTER, TIFFANY, WHO WAS KILLED ON
OCTOBER 25, 1995, WHEN HER SCHOOL BUS WAS STRUCK BY A TRAIN IN FOX RIVER GROVE. A YEAR LATER,
PLASTIC ANGELS STILL HUNG FROM A TREE TO HONOR THE SEVEN TEENAGERS KILLED IN THE ACCIDENT.

FIRST CHAMPIONSHIP. PHOTO BY BRIAN JACKSON, JUNE 12, 1991
MICHAEL JORDAN CLUTCHES THE NBA CHAMPIONSHIP TROPHY AFTER THE BULLS BEAT THE LAKERS 4 GAMES TO 1.
HIS FATHER, JAMES, IS TO HIS RIGHT. "I'M NUMB," JORDAN SAID.

RIGHT: BAD AS HE WANTS TO BE. PHOTO BY BRIAN JACKSON, MAY 4, 1996
DENNIS RODMAN SHOWS UP AT A MICHIGAN AVENUE BOOK SIGNING IN ANYTHING BUT HIS UNIFORM.

ESCAPE FROM EXPLOSION. PHOTO BY JOHN H. WHITE, OCTOBER 30, 1998
PEOPLE FLEE FLAMES AND HEAT AFTER A NATURAL GAS PIPE IGNITED NEAR A CHA APARTMENT BUILDING.

DEEP THOUGHTS. PHOTO BY AL PODGORSKI, AUGUST 19, 1997
WORKERS STAND IN THE DEEP TUNNEL, CHICAGO'S LARGEST PUBLIC WORKS PROJECT, BENEATH SUBURBAN RIVER GROVE

A SHOW OF HANDS. PHOTO BY KEITH HALE, AUGUST 22, 2002
PRANITA JAIN BRINGS ANCIENT DANCE FROM HER INDIAN HOMELAND TO HER NEW CHICAGO HOME.

FACES IN A CROWD. PHOTO BY TOM CRUZE, APRIL 15, 2002
AMY TORRES-FREESE GIVES HER YORKSHIRE TERRIER A LIFT AS SHE BLADES ALONG THE LAKEFRONT.

SOUNDS OF SILENCE. PHOTO BY PABLO MARTINEZ MONSIVAIS, FEBRUARY 20, 1997
LUCINDA CARVER CONDUCTS AN ORCHESTRA TO ACCOMPANY THE 1928 SILENT MOVIE "THE PASSION OF JOAN OF
ARC." THE PERFORMANCE WAS AT THE MEDINAH TEMPLE.

The cows come home. Photo by Al Podgorski, June 15, 1999
Mayor Richard M. Daley kicks off the wildly successful "Cows on Parade" public art exhibition.

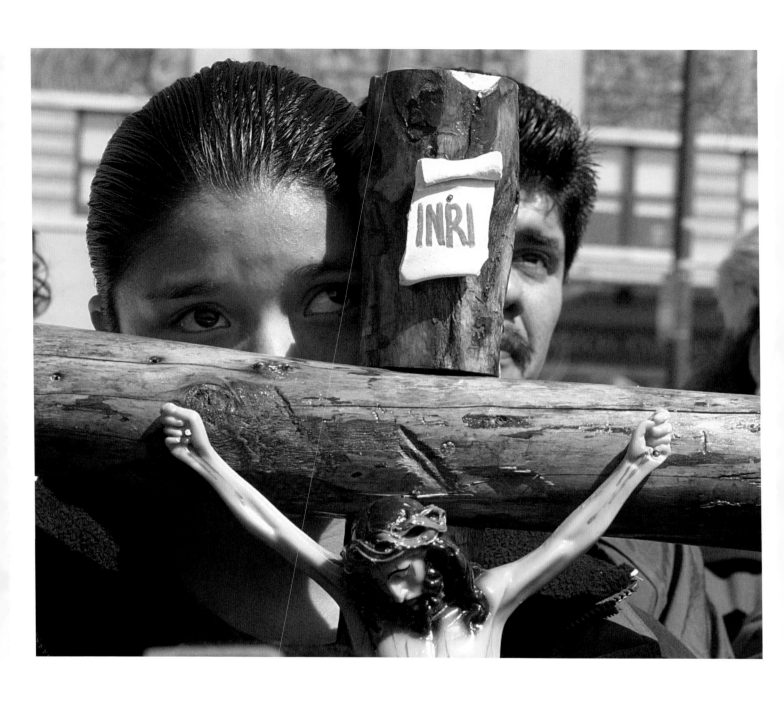

GOOD FRIDAY. PHOTO BY JOHN H. WHITE, APRIL 13, 2001
MARICRUZ GAYTAN TAKES PART IN THE ANNUAL WAY OF THE CROSS PROCESSION THROUGH PILSEN.

'TODAY WE GRIEVE.' PHOTO BY JEAN LACHAT, DECEMBER 27, 2000
MEGAN CONLON JOINS FAMILY AND FRIENDS AT THE FUNERAL OF SCOTT GILLEN, A FIREFIGHTER KILLED BY A
MOTORIST AT AN EMERGENCY SCENE. CONLON, HOLDING THE HELMET, WAS GILLEN'S STEPDAUGHTER.

GOOD SPIRITS. PHOTO BY ROBERT A. DAVIS, JANUARY 24, 1993
A DRAGON DANCER HELPS RING IN THE NEW YEAR ON SOUTH WENTWORTH AVENUE IN CHINATOWN.

Dancing in the sun. Photo by Richard A. Chapman, July 25, 2003

Pilsen residents fill the streets for the Fiesta del Sol.

SEPTEMBER 11, 2001. PHOTO BY RICH HEIN

SEPTEMBER 11, 2001. PHOTO BY BRIAN JACKSON

SEPTEMBER 11, 2001. PHOTO BY TOM CRUZE

Mowing them down. Photo by Richard A. Chapman, September 12, 2003
Kerry Wood dusts back Cincinnati Reds Juan Castro during the pennant-stretch run.

A TITLE AT LAST. PHOTO BY JON SALL, SEPTEMBER 27, 2003
SAMMY SOSA CELEBRATES AS THE CUBS CLINCH THEIR FIRST DIVISION TITLE IN 14 YEARS.

IRAQ PROTEST. PHOTO BY JOHN J. KIM, MARCH 20, 2004
POLICE IN RIOT GEAR ARE SEEN THROUGH A TORN U.S. FLAG DURING AN ANTI-WAR RALLY.

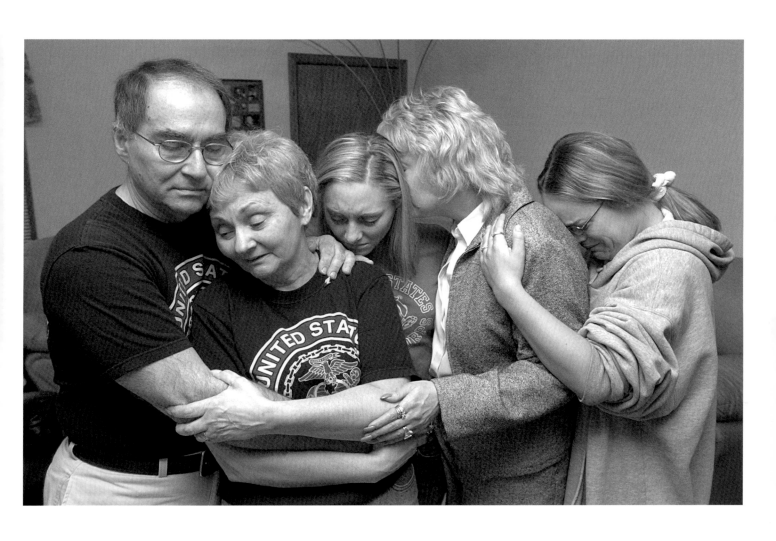

Death hits home. Photo by Rich Hein, April 13, 2004
The family of Marine Lance Corporal Phil Frank support each other while talking about
how he died in Iraq. From left, they are Phil's father, Roy; mother Georgette; sister Cyndi;
and cousins Robin Van Cleave and Kristin Van Cleave.

THE SHELL OF A MAN. PHOTO BY RICHARD A. CHAPMAN, SEPTEMBER 9, 2003
ARCHITECT FRANK GEHRY TALKS AND WALKS AS HE SHOWS OFF HIS MILLENIUM PARK MUSIC SHELL.

FINALLY. PHOTO BY RICHARD A. CHAPMAN, AUGUST 3, 2004
CHILDREN PLAY IN THE WADING SECTION OF THE PARK'S CROWN FOUNTAIN AFTER ITS LONG-DELAYED OPENING.